VEGAN CHINESE FOOD

YANG LIU

VEGAN CHINESE FOOD

YANG LIU

PHOTOGRAPHS BY KATHARINA PINCZOLITS

Hardie Grant

BOOKS

This book is more than a cookbook. It is not simply a collection of traditional Chinese recipes and the history behind them, but a homage to the food I grew up eating and the memories and people connected to it. These are the recipes I learned from my grandmother, my aunt and my mother, and developed myself.

I want to show you that it is possible to cook plant-based Chinese dishes that are every bit as delicious as mainstream Chinese food. Vegan food was a part of Chinese cuisine long before it arrived in many other parts of the world. It was not a trend, but the way people ate for hundreds of years. For that reason, there is a whole chapter dedicated to the history of veganism in China, dating back to Ancient China.

This cookbook and the recipes in it are also connected to my personal story. I am sharing with you dishes from all the different regions I have lived in China. You will find traditional recipes from Beijing to Chengdu, from Changhsha to Guangzhou. There will be an introduction to the main sauces and condiments in China, and I really hope the variations of tofu dishes, stir-fries, noodles and desserts will allow you a glimpse into the vast world of vegan Chinese cuisine.

MY STORY

Food has always been very close to my heart. It is much more than just fuel; it has a lot of sentimental value and is closely tied to memories and my identity. I was born in the early nineties in a town of 8 million people in Hunan province, which is probably the spiciest region of China. Food played an integral role in my upbringing, and is connected to most of my memories of childhood. Like everyone from Hunan, I was introduced to spicy food at a very early age, and started eating it daily when I was around two years old. We used to have spicy fresh rice noodles for breakfast, which is, to this day, still my all-time favourite dish.

In Hunan I lived with my grandmother, my aunt and her children, my two older cousins. When I think about my grandmother I always remember the bucket of sweet snacks that she stored next to her cupboard. Most of them tasted horrible. I remember particularly well a package of sugared ginger, but those snacks were still special for my cousins and me, as we didn't have many others to share at that time. My grandma would always save the snacks for later. Sometimes they had expired for weeks or even months, but she didn't want to get rid of them.

Besides the spicy rice noodles for breakfast, my grandma's snacks and the very good food my aunt and uncle cooked at home, there were so many street foods I recall from my early childhood. A perfect summer night back then was buying an iced jelly downstairs, having dinner at home, then going out to have different flavours of shaved ice, then on to a barbecue stand. It is very common in China to go out a few hours after dinner to enjoy a late-night snack (especially in summer). This late-night meal is called 'siu yeh' (宵夜). In Hunan, barbecued food is the go-to siu yeh for most people.

Most homes in the south of China don't have heating systems, although it can get extremely cold in the winter. We had a coal stove for cooking and a small electric heater at home. I remember that the coal stove was always placed in the middle of the room, and we would put the fire tongs on the stove and grill Hunanese sticky rice cake over it, watching the cake getting larger and rounder as it heated. The once-hard rice cake became tender and sticky after grilling, and we would share it while sitting by the stove. Hot food, like a bowl of spicy rice noodles or wontons, was extra comforting in winter, and it helped us to get through the coldest days.

Sharing every meal and snacks with my family, playing Mah Jiang and running around with my cousins were key features of my early childhood. I also supported my grandmother and my aunt by going to the markets to get fresh groceries. During this time I learned how to pick the fruits and vegetables, and all the tricks my cousins and aunts taught me to find the best harvest.

The Hunanese food of my childhood formed my earliest culinary memories and laid the foundation for my love of food. After living in Hunan with my grandmother for some years, I moved with my mum to Guangzhou when I was six, which is the capital city of Guangdong (Canton) province.

Arriving in Guangzhou, I was exposed to a completely different environment and culture, and also very different food. No one spoke Mandarin at school, not even the Chinese teacher, since everyone mainly spoke Cantonese. My start in Guangzhou was not the easiest, but fortunately I learned Cantonese quickly. On my way home from school, I would always get different street foods and snacks, then go to the market to get groceries for dinner.

In general, Cantonese cuisine is mild in taste and has absolutely nothing to do with spicy food. You could almost say that I went from the spiciest region of China to the least spicy one. It was completely different to what I was used to, and though I never lost my love for spicy food, I soon also grew to love the rich Cantonese cuisine, especially the enormous

variety of dim sums. There is a famous Chinese saying, '食在廣州', which basically means 'there's nothing but good food in Guangzhou'.

To this date, yum cha is still my favourite kind of meal. Yum cha is a Cantonese sort of brunch with a huge variety of dim sums to choose from – many restaurants offer one hundred or more, and there are, in total, more than a thousand different kinds.

Being raised by a single mum was unusual and difficult at times. I was very often home alone while she was working, and because of that I started to prepare my own food at a very young age. I think I cooked my first real dish when I was seven years old. It was pan-fried tofu with fresh chilli, a very typical Hunanese home dish, which my aunt made frequently. I learned how to cook primarily from my grandparents, my mum, my aunts and uncles, but especially from the aunt I lived with in my earliest years and her husband, who ran several small restaurants over the years.

Growing up in Guangzhou also exposed me to a huge variety of street foods and, over the years, whenever I met up with friends, we would always go for food together. In fact, I would say that eating with friends was the theme of my social life.

I have travelled to many regions in China, mostly during my Bachelor's studies, and I lived in Sichuan for 6 months when I was a volunteer teacher there. I also spent some time in Beijing while studying Spanish. But a common feature of all of my travels has been an exploration of authentic local food. In Sichuan I learned some of the most typical dishes of that region, like a hot pot paste, made from scratch.

After my studies in China I decided to go to Spain to continue studying Spanish. I lived in Salamanca for one year, then in Barcelona, where I finished my Master's degree. During my time in Spain I honed my cooking skills a lot by cooking every day and hosting regular dinner parties, as I missed Chinese food and there were no authentic Chinese restaurants around.

Ten years ago I converted to Buddhism, but I was drawn to the idea of veganism long before that. I was twelve when I first attempted to go vegan, but it failed after two weeks because the adults in my family wouldn't allow it, most of them believing that it was only healthy to eat both meat and vegetables.

I was first properly introduced to Buddhism when I stayed at a Buddhist temple with a friend of my mum's for three days. It was almost like a retreat: we ate the vegan food at the temple, talked to the monks, listened to the lectures and attended some rituals. And ever since then the Buddhist belief that 'all lives are equal' has really stuck with me. In 2016, I became a strict vegetarian and cut out all meat and fish from my diet, but in my heart I knew that I would become vegan one day.

I met Kathi not long after I became vegetarian, in the summer of 2016. We actually met by chance in a phone shop. Kathi was in the line ahead of me and had a problem with her roaming and I helped her out. Afterwards, we walked home to her dorm, which was around the corner from my apartment. On that short walk, we were talking and immediately connected on so many levels. Among other things, Kathi actually went to Guangzhou for her exchange semester during her Bachelor studies, exactly at the time when I left Guangzhou to go to Spain. She too was amazed by the rich variety of Chinese food and especially loved Cantonese cuisine. And besides that, I was planning to visit my best friend in Austria, the country Kathi was born and raised in. We started joking that we could fly together to Austria and, funnily enough, this actually did happen 2 months later. After my studies, I moved to Vienna to live with Kathi, and after a while we both became vegan.

A very special moment for us was in 2018 when we flew to China together to visit my mum and relatives. We travelled to Guangzhou, my hometown in Hunan and also to the capital city in Hunan, Changsha. For both of us it was the first time we'd returned to China since 2015. We visited so many new vegan restaurants and had so much amazing food, but we were most impressed by a restaurant located inside a Buddhist temple where they served a vegan buffet of more than two hundred options. Neither of us had ever experienced anything like that before, especially not with vegan food. In Austria, often the only vegan option on a restaurant menu was salad, so the variety of options and the meat substitutes just did not compare.

It was such a nice experience to show Kathi all the places I used to go to in my hometown and all the food I grew up eating. Of course, we tried the spicy rice noodles there, which are now also Kathi's favourite food. There was one day when we had them for breakfast, lunch and dinner.

In 2019, Kathi and I started our Instagram channel quite spontaneously. The previous Christmas, we had hosted a charity cooking event in a city close to Vienna, and we planned to host another one that autumn. Many of the people who had attended asked us if we worked for a restaurant, and Kathi suggested that it would be great if people were able to find us online. So, two weeks before the event, we opened our Instagram account. For the name we decided to go with our favourite food in the world – littlericenoodle.

In the beginning, we just shared pictures of the dishes I veganised, but we received such interest in our food that we soon started sharing recipes and cooking videos as well. Kathi manages our Instagram account and takes the pictures and videos, and I focus on the recipe development and cooking. It has been such a joy and blessing to share our love and passion for both Chinese food and vegan food, and to connect with people around the world. We hope that this book inspires you to give vegan food a try too.

A BRIEF HISTORY OF VEGANISM IN CHINA

Many people assume that veganism is a relatively new trend that began in the West and filtered into other parts of the world. But, in fact, there are many countries like China that have a long history of veganism dating back hundreds or even thousands of years.

Throughout most of their history, the vast majority of people in China lived off a largely plant-based diet – simply because there was no other option. Compared to the scattered nomads that lived in peripheral regions, for whom meat and dairy were central to their diet, most of the Chinese population were peasants who could not afford or have regular access to meat and dairy products. They might have kept a few hens, one or two pigs and a cow, but these animals were too precious for them to eat. They needed the hens to produce eggs, which they normally used to trade other necessities; they needed the cattle to plough the fields, and the pigs were kept for selling, which also made up a significant part of their income. For many, eating meat was a luxury they could only afford once a year, and this was the norm for many Chinese people until just a few decades ago. My mum always tells me that when she was growing up in the sixties and seventies – even until the early eighties – the only time she ate meat was at Chinese New Year. They could not even afford to eat rice every day and mostly lived off the sweet potatoes my grandfather grew. For years afterwards, my mum never wanted to eat sweet potato, but she has gradually learned to appreciate it again.

For a long time, the Chinese diet was based mainly on the vegetables, plants and fruits that peasants grew and foraged, until the invention of tofu changed the whole picture. Tofu and other soybean products soon became the most important and versatile ingredients of vegan Chinese cooking. There are many theories on the origin of tofu, but the most popular one is that tofu was invented around 141 BC by Prince Liu An of the Han Dynasty. For over two thousand years, it has been the main source of protein for most of the Chinese population. In the book *Qimin Yaoshu* (齊民要術), by Sixie Jia, which is often referred to as the 'Encyclopedia of Ancient China', eleven vegan recipes were recorded. The book was completed between 533 and 544 AD, which makes these the oldest vegan recipes known in China. One chapter of the book describes the cooking of eggplant (aubergine), winter melon (wax melon), calabash leaves, sweetened ginger, fermented beans, nori and other plant-based ingredients.

Emperor Wu (464–549 AD) of the Liang Dynasty, also known as Xiao Yan, was the person who laid the foundation of veganism in Chinese Buddhism. Shortly after becoming emperor, he converted to Buddhism and in an announcement he outlawed the consumption of meat and alcohol for Buddhist monks. In another announcement he banned animal sacrifices at ancestral temples (Jongmyo). Before that only the consumption of alcohol and garlic was forbidden in Chinese Buddhism and eating meat was not strictly banned.

Given that one of the basic concepts of Buddhism is that 'all lives are equal', Buddhist monks in China have, since the sixth century, lived as strict vegans. With the widespread adoption of Buddhism in the following centuries, vegan food was increasingly accepted by the upper class of society who could afford to eat meat every day.

When talking about vegan food in Ancient China, it's easy to assume that the only options were plain vegetables and rice, but there is evidence that vegan meat substitutes (often prepared with soybeans or gluten) have formed a large part of traditional Chinese cuisine for many, many years. In the book *The Eastern Capital: A Dream of Splendor* (東京夢華錄), by Meng Yuanlao, written in the mid-twelfth century, substitutes such as vegan fish and vegan clams were documented. Another book,

Meng Liang Lu (夢粱錄), by Wu Zimu, which recorded life in the late thirteenth century in the capital city Lin An of the Southern Song Dynasty, vegan or vegetarian dim sum restaurants were mentioned, along with the names of twenty-eight vegan or vegetarian dim sums, including baozi filled with a vegan meat substitute.

Meat substitutes made from calabash and gluten were first documented in the cookbook *Shanjia qinggong* (山家清供), by Lin Hong, written between the twelfth and the thirteenth centuries, along with more than eighty other vegan foods, including flowers, sweets, fruits and soybean products. A vegan cookbook from the same era, *Benxin Vegan Cookbook* (本心齋疏食譜), by Chen Dasou, documented twenty simple recipes, such as the cooking of tofu, lotus roots, yams, goji berries, chestnuts, garlic chives and pickled vegetables.

Vegan Chinese cuisine developed greatly after the thirteenth century, reaching its prime in the late Qing Dynasty when it could be roughly divided into three categories.

The first was vegan palace food. During some special days, rituals or festivals, the emperor and empress needed to eat vegan as a tradition, and there was a vegan kitchen in the Forbidden City responsible for preparing this food. Vegan palace food was rich and extravagant, and given the complexity of many of the dishes and the expensive ingredients needed to make them, it was only consumed by a select few people, and formed only a small part of traditional vegan Chinese food.

The second kind was temple food – the food cooked by Buddhist monks, not only for themselves to eat, but also to offer to the visitors at the temple. Temple food mostly involved natural and common ingredients cooked using simple methods, and since many Buddhist temples grew their own vegetables and grains, they cooked what they had to hand. However, ginger and everything from the allium family, including garlic and spring onion (scallion), were strictly avoided, as in Buddhism it is believed the bad smell of these foods and their negative impact on the body could disturb one's Buddhist practice.

Temple food was a big part of traditional vegan food, but it was not limited only to the temples. Many temples and Buddhists opened their own Buddhist restaurants, and vegan meat substitutes made with ingredients such as soybeans, seitan and konjac could be found in many dishes they offered. When I was living with my aunt, she used to go to the Buddhist temple almost every week to attend the rituals. Afterwards she would always bring back delicious vegan food cooked by the monks and the common Buddhists who helped out at the temple. Some of the foods I remember most vividly were the spicy rice noodles made with mushrooms and bamboo shoots, vegan drumsticks made with tofu sheets braised in a spicy sauce, and dumplings filled with all kinds of vegetables. I still remember how I shared the food with my cousins at the table and told my aunt to bring more next time; it feels like yesterday.

The third kind was the common vegan food, which was eaten and cooked by most people and formed the majority of traditional vegan Chinese food. As well as the vegan food people cooked in their homes, vegan restaurants were also opening, offering new and inventive dishes that took their influence from palace and temple food as well.

I think the first time I went to a vegan restaurant was about twenty years ago. Back then there weren't so many, and most of them were Buddhist restaurants, which have a strong focus on recreating traditional dishes with vegan meat substitutes. When I went back to China the last time, in 2019, I was amazed by how many new and innovative vegan restaurants there were. I tried so many creative dishes that I had never eaten before, and all of them composites of palace, temple and common vegan food, prepared using the diverse cooking methods of different regions in China and around the world.

In *A Brief Introduction to Vegan Food* (素食說略), by Xue Baochen, which was completed in the early twentieth century, more than 170 vegan recipes were documented, from the making of basic condiments, such as soy sauce, rice vinegar, pickled vegetables, fermented beans, fermented tofu and chilli sauce, to the cooking of all kinds of vegetables, tofu, noodles, pastries, soups and even rare mushrooms. It also included a very interesting recipe for vegan ham, which was prepared by filling a very ripe pumpkin with aged soy sauce, then hanging it under the roof for 7 months before steaming and slicing it. It is described as 'very tasty and healthy'. The author, Xue Baochen, wrote in the preface of the book, 'Vegan food is rich in flavor, which is not only refreshing and delicious, but also good for one's health. One can appreciate the pleasure of life when birds can fly and fish can swim freely. Veganism does not only make one enjoy food more, but also increases one's happiness. This is the most fundamental meaning of veganism'.

PLEASE NOTE

This book uses 15 ml (½ fl oz) tablespoons. Cooks using 20 ml (¾ fl oz) tablespoons should be scant with their tablespoon measurements. Metric cup measurements are used, i.e. 250 ml for 1 cup; in the US a cup is 8 fl oz, just smaller, so American cooks should be generous in their cup measurements. Additionally, the recipes in this book were cooked in a fan-forced or convection oven, so if using a conventional oven increase the temperature by 20°C (35°F).

Finally, sugar hasn't been specified as all instances refer simply to normal granulated cane sugar unless otherwise specified.

TIPS ON HOW TO USE THIS BOOK

THE CONCEPT OF FOOD SHARING IN CHINA

As in many other Asian countries, for every meal in China multiple dishes are always shared between families and friends, rather than everyone having a plate of their own food. The unspoken rule is normally to have as many dishes as the number of people eating, plus one. For example, if three people go to a restaurant, they would normally order four dishes.

Besides the sauces and condiments, most of the recipes in this book are for two people to share, if not stated otherwise. If you are only cooking for one or two people, the easiest and quickest option would be to make either dumplings (such as the Spicy sour soup dumplings on page 185 or the Sesame paste dumplings on page 187), fried rice (Soy sauce fried rice is the most classic and easy one, on page 179) or noodles (like my Spring onion oil noodles, page 170, or Mushroom chow fun, page 173).

If you plan to prepare a nice meal for your family or friends, it would be good to include one tofu dish, one or two dishes of your preferred vegetables, one dish of leafy greens, fried rice or noodles, a drink and a dessert. If I were to choose some dishes from this cookbook for a dinner for five, I would probably make Mapo tofu (page 61), Dry-fried green beans (page 104), Yuxiang eggplant (page 91), Sweet and sour lotus root (page 118), Stir-fried water spinach (page 131) and Hong Kong supreme soy sauce fried noodles (page 175), with Hong Kong lemon tea (page 199) as a drink and Mango pomelo sago (page 209) for dessert.

MEASUREMENTS AND INGREDIENTS

All cooking times given are approximate. The exact cooking time will differ depending on which stove you use, how strong the heat is and which cooking utensils you use. It is much more important to observe the state of the ingredients rather than working to a timer. For example, I normally stir-fry chopped garlic for 30 seconds before adding other ingredients, but if you have a very strong flame and the garlic is turning golden after 20 seconds, the next ingredient should be added at this point. Or if your flame is weak and the garlic only becomes fragrant after 1 minute, then the cooking time of every step should be stretched.

The amount of oil in the recipes is also simply a guide, because it depends on how much you normally use for cooking and on the cooking equipment you have. If you have a non-stick wok or pan, then not much oil is needed for cooking, but if you don't have a good wok or pan, you might need to add some extra oil to prevent sticking.

Canola oil, corn oil, peanut oil and soybean oil can be used as the normal cooking oil in all the recipes. All of these oils have a high smoking point, which is essential for the stir-frying, pan-frying and deep-frying we do most often in Chinese cooking. Avoid using oils that have a particularly low smoking point, such as extra-virgin olive oil or linseed oil. When these oils smoke, they become unstable and create harmful chemicals.

As for the measurements, you can of course adjust a little to your taste and depending on the products you have. Different brands of soy sauce vary in taste and saltiness, and this also applies to many other sauces.

PRODUCT RECOMMENDATIONS

This book could not fit a comprehensive list of sauces and products we buy in the supermarket or in the Asian grocer. So, instead, we have provided an up-to-date shopping guide on our website. Just visit littlericenoodle.com/cookbook-recommendations.

Chinese cuisine has a history of thousands of years, and many traditional cooking techniques and skills are barely used nowadays, while others developed over time and are still widely used in modern Chinese cooking. Here, I would like to give a short introduction to eleven of the most common cooking techniques and the concept of Wok Hei in Chinese cooking.

CHINESE COOKING TECHNIQUES

STIR-FRYING

(炒) Stir-frying is definitely the most basic and common cooking technique in Chinese cooking. For stir-frying, the ingredients are usually cut into slices, strips or small chunks. First, heat a wok over a medium-high heat, then add some oil, followed by the ingredients. Keep stirring the ingredients and tossing the wok to avoid burning. The ingredients should be cooked in a relatively short time.

There are many different kinds of stir-frying depending on the different ingredients and oil temperatures, including raw stir-frying (生炒), which is to stir-fry raw ingredients directly until fully cooked; cooked stir-frying (熟炒), which is to stir-fry ingredients that have already been cooked; smooth stir-frying (滑炒), which is to first cook marinated or battered ingredients quickly in oil (the oil temperature should not be very hot) before stir-frying them; and plain stir-frying (清炒), which is to stir-fry the main ingredient quickly with very few side ingredients (often only garlic) and is used mostly to cook leafy greens, usually seasoned only with salt.

DEEP-FRYING

(炸) Deep-frying is a common cooking method in many cuisines. Food is submerged in hot oil and cooked over a high heat, normally until it's golden-brown and crispy. There are different kinds of deep-frying in Chinese cooking. Dry deep-frying (乾炸) is to first marinate the ingredients and coat them with batter, flour or starch before deep-frying twice. Foods fried with this method are usually golden, crunchy and a bit dry on the outside. Soft deep-frying (軟炸) involves dipping the ingredients in a batter normally made with eggs, flour and starch, then deep-frying them twice with a lower oil temperature than that of dry deep-frying. Crispy deep-frying (酥炸) is when ingredients are first cooked or steamed before being deep-fried (with or without batter).

PAN-FRYING

(煎) Pan-frying is another very common cooking method involving frying food in oil – usually more oil than in stir-frying – until it's golden and crispy on the outside. It is similar to deep-frying but requires much less oil, and therefore takes a bit more time. For panfrying, ingredients are normally prepared flat or sliced, and when one side is evenly fried, they are turned and cooked on the other side until they're golden and cooked through. In Chinese cooking, pan-frying is often the first step to 'process' the ingredients before they are cooked again using another method. For example, tofu is very often pan-fried before it's cooked together with other ingredients because the taste and texture of tofu are much improved after pan-frying.

BAO-FRYING

(爆炒) Bao (爆) means explosive and fierce in Chinese. Bao-frying involves first heating up a wok until it's extremely hot, then adding oil and stir-frying ingredients over the highest heat possible. The cooking process is very short, and in order for the ingredients to be cooked quickly, they must be cut into small pieces or thinly sliced. There are several bao-frying methods. The first is to cook the ingredients in hot oil, then season with a few condiments. Leek bao-frying involves first adding some leek to the hot oil before adding other ingredients. This brings a special taste and aroma to the dish. And, finally, sauce bao-frying is to bao-fry the ingredients in hot oil and sauces.

QUICK-FRYING

(熘) Quick-frying is generally to first marinate and cook the ingredients quickly (by deep-frying, steaming or boiling), then quickly stir-fry the ingredients with the sauce and other condiments, adding a little water mixed with starch at the end to thicken the sauce. Otherwise you can prepare the sauce – thickened with water and starch – in a separate pan while the ingredients are being cooked (normally deep-fried), then pour the sauce over the cooked ingredients. Traditionally, sweet-sour (糖醋) dishes are cooked with this technique.

STEAMING

(蒸) Steaming is a cooking method in which water vapour is used as a heat conductor. The ingredients are placed above but separate from the water and cooked over a high or medium heat. Common steaming methods include plain steaming (清蒸), which is to steam the ingredients and season them simply at the end of the steaming, often with soy sauce and hot oil. Wrapped steaming (包蒸) is to wrap the ingredients, normally with lotus leaves or leafy greens, before steaming. Ground rice steaming (粉蒸) is very common in some southern provinces, like Hunan, Hubei and Jiangxi, and involves first toasting glutinous rice with spices and grinding everything together, then coating the ingredients with the ground rice before steaming.

Steaming is viewed by many as the healthiest cooking method, as the nutrients of the food can be best preserved through steaming. The city of Liuyang in Hunan province is very famous for its steaming cooking methods. Most of its local dishes require steaming in the cooking process.

BOILING

(煮) Boiling is a very simple cooking method employed by every cuisine around the world. Although it is usually as simple as cooking ingredients over a high heat in soup or water, in Chinese cooking it is not as boring as it sounds. Many dishes are cooked in soups of all different flavours. For example, in Sichuan cuisine, ingredients are cooked in a spicy soup seasoned with Pixian broad bean paste (see page 26), dried chilli and other spices, and hot oil is poured over the dish at the end.

BRAISING

(燒) Braising means to first pan-fry or stir-fry ingredients, then add soup or water and condiments. First, bring the soup to the boil over a high heat, then reduce the heat to medium–low and cook the ingredients until they become soft and tender. For some braised dishes, it is also necessary to thicken the sauce with a little water mixed with starch at the end. Based on the difference in taste, colour and amount of sauce, braising can be divided into red braising (紅燒), white braising (白燒), dry braising (乾燒), sauced braising (醬燒) and leek braising (蔥燒). The most commonly used is red braising, which is to first pan-fry or deep-fry the main ingredient, then cook it slowly with Chinese cooking wine, soy sauce, other condiments and broth or water. The finished dish is red or deep red in colour, hence the name.

STEWING

(炖) Stewing and braising are similar techniques. The difference is that stewed dishes have more sauce or soup than braised dishes. There are two kinds of stewing. One involves cooking the main ingredient first in boiling water before you heat oil in a wok or clay pot, add leek, ginger and the main ingredients, then add the soup or water, cooking it slowly over a medium–low heat. The second kind of stewing is combined with steaming. It is to have the seasoned ingredients (normally with soup) in a container, like a clay bowl, covered with a lid and placed in a steaming pot. Many soups are stewed in this way since it is believed this method can best preserve the flavours and nutrients of a soup, but it can take a few hours to prepare.

SIMMERING

(燜) Simmering is also similar to braising, but it takes longer and requires a lower heat. Simmering is to first cook the ingredients (by stir-frying, pan-frying, boiling, etc.), then add sauce and condiments, put the lid on the pot or wok and cook the food slowly over a low heat. Some simmered dishes need to be cooked for hours, keeping the temperature just around boiling point. This method is typically used for ingredients that require long, slow cooking to achieve the best flavour and texture.

ROASTING

(烤) As in other cuisines, roasting in Chinese cooking usually involves marinating, seasoning and then cooking the ingredients over a grill or in an oven. Roasting requires a higher cooking temperature compared to most other cooking methods, and it is the method used in many traditional dishes like Peking duck. During roasting, the moisture on the surface of the ingredients evaporates, resulting in a crispy outer layer, while the internal moisture is retained. This method brings out a very unique flavour in the food. Roasted food is typically served with a dipping sauce, or it could be cooked again using other cooking techniques.

WOK HEI

(鑊氣) Wok Hei is a basic concept in Cantonese cooking, which translates literally into 'the air of the wok'. The term refers to the distinct fragrance and charred, smoky flavour of foods that have been stir-fried quickly over a strong open flame. Many theories explain Wok Hei with the Maillard reaction: a chemical reaction that happens between amino acids and reducing sugars over very high temperatures, which gives browned food (like fried dumplings or toasted bread) its distinctive flavour. Typically, when soy sauce is being added to a wok of ingredients over high heat, the sugar in the soy sauce caramelises instantly. The amino acids and reducing sugars react with each other and bring out the unique smell and taste, which forms the main part of Wok Hei.

In order to obtain Wok Hei, the wok has to first be heated up until it's very hot, then the ingredients must be cooked over a strong flame in a very short time to avoid burning and to cook more evenly. Everything must be stirred and tossed constantly. The most representative Cantonese dish with Wok Hei is beef chow fun (乾炒牛河), but we have created a vegan Mushroom chow fun (page 173) for this book.

If you are serious about cooking great Chinese food, you need a good wok. Many people are not aware that seasoning and caring for a wok is more important than spending a lot of money on a nice one. Even a good-quality wok can become sticky, rusty and inconvenient to use if it is not properly maintained.

Traditionally, the main piece of cooking equipment in Chinese cooking is a wok made of wrought iron. A wrought-iron wok is much lighter than a cast-iron wok or pot, and it conducts heat very quickly and evenly. It is also easier for the cook to flip, which makes it ideal for cooking quick stir-fried dishes over a high heat. Most of the iron woks on the market now are made with carbon steel. It is very similar to wrought iron but it contains a higher percentage of carbon.

Iron woks do not come with a non-stick coating, and despite the wok's smooth-looking surface, there are actually many tiny 'pores' on it. This is particularly problematic when cooking proteins and starches, such as meat, eggs, tofu, potatoes, lotus roots, etc. The starch and protein in these foods instantly denature and deteriorate when heated. The denatured part is absorbed and caught by the little 'pores' of the wok, which is why ingredients stick to woks or pans. Therefore, it is very important to season the wok before first cooking anything in it. Seasoning creates a non-stick coating, an 'oil film' that fills the 'pores' and protects the ingredients from getting caught. If the maintenance is done the right way, you will have the best cooking pal for many years to come.

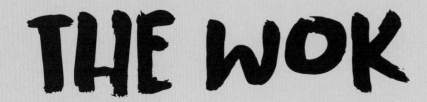

THE WOK

SEASONING THE WOK

A new wok normally comes waxed or coated with industrial oil, which is harmful to both your health and the wok itself if it isn't removed. First, add some lukewarm water and a bit of dishwashing detergent and use the rough side of a kitchen sponge to thoroughly scrub the wax or oil off. Rinse well. Dry the inside and outside of the wok, then heat it over the highest heat possible (preferably on a gas stove), tilting the wok constantly to make sure all of its surface is heated evenly. The wok will first turn dark, then red, then blue-purple. When it becomes blue, turn off the heat and add about 100 ml (3½ fl oz) oil (peanut, canola or corn oil is best), rotating and tilting the wok so that the surface is evenly coated by the oil. Pour the oil out and dry the inside of the wok with paper towel.

Now, set the wok over the lowest heat, dip a paper towel into some fresh oil and, holding it with chopsticks or tongs, rub the paper towel evenly over the inner surface of the wok. After a few seconds, remove the wok from the heat and dry with a paper towel. Repeat this step eight to ten times. It sounds like a lot, but the more this step is repeated, the better the initial 'oil film' will be. Turn off the heat and rub the wok with a fresh paper towel one last time on the inside and outside, then leave the wok to cool. Wait at least 12 hours after seasoning your wok before using it, to allow the oil to seep into the 'pores' and form an 'oil film'.

Before first use, rinse the wok under lukewarm water and dry it with a soft tea towel (dish towel) or paper towel. Heat the wok over a high heat, and after about 30 seconds, add cool (room-temperature) oil, tilting the wok quickly so it's evenly coated with oil, then add your ingredients. This technique is called 'Hot wok cool oil' and it's used frequently in Chinese cooking to prevent burning and sticking. If the wok and the oil are both very hot, ingredients can easily burn and stick to the wok. If the wok and oil are both cold when you place it over a high heat, then thermal expansion will cause the parts of the ingredients directly in contact with the wok to burn quickly, resulting in singed edges, while the centres of the ingredients remain uncooked.

MAINTAINING THE WOK

It's best not to clean a wok right after cooking while it is still very hot. Wait until it has cooled down naturally, and especially do not add cold water to a hot wok; the instant thermal expansion and contraction will damage the protective coating that has been built. If you must clean the wok immediately after cooking, add hot water and use a kitchen brush or sponge.

Once the wok has cooled down, if there is only some oil or sauce left in the wok, first clean it with paper towel, then rinse it under warm/hot water before drying with a soft tea towel (dish towel). It is very important to dry the wok after it comes in contact with water, otherwise it will start to rust after only a few hours. After cleaning, the routine care for a wok is to heat it up again over the lowest heat. Once hot, turn off the heat and rub a little oil on the surface of the wok to strengthen the 'oil film'. It is not recommended to use dishwashing detergent or a dishwasher to clean a wok, or any abrasive cleaning products like steel wool. If there is something hard or burnt that's sticking to the wok, first soak it in hot water for half an hour, then try to rub it off with a kitchen brush or sponge.

Every time a wok is used and cleaned properly, the oil from cooking keeps filling the 'pores' of the wok and maintains the 'oil film'. After it has been used a few times, the colour of the wok should turn darker, but the surface should become shinier. If you use a wok a lot to boil water or to cook acidic ingredients, such as vinegar, lemon juice or tomatoes, the surface of the wok might become dull again. Simply complete the routine care: heat up the wok, then turn the heat off and rub a thin layer of oil on the wok with paper towel, then let it rest overnight.

SAUCES

In this chapter I share some of the common sauces and condiments used in Chinese cooking, and how to make them from scratch. Having home-made sauces to hand can really help a lot with cooking and make dishes unique with a personal touch.

Before sharing how to prepare some of these classic sauces, I would like to briefly introduce the most basic and fundamental sauces and condiments that are commonly used in Chinese cooking. The first step towards cooking authentic Chinese food is to have the right sauces and spices.

A tip for when you go shopping for Chinese sauces and condiments is to look out for these signs. The Chinese signs '素' and '素食' are broad terms that include both vegetarianism and veganism. 'Vegan' in Chinese is '純素' or '全素', but many Chinese confuse vegetarianism and veganism and, as a result, many of the vegan sauces you will find in Asian grocery stores are not strictly labelled. Very often, the English name of the sauce says 'vegetarian', but it is actually vegan, so always check.

SOY SAUCE

(醤油) Soy sauce literally means 'sauce' (醤) and 'oil' (油) in Chinese, although no oil is added in the production process. Soy sauce has been the most fundamental condiment in Chinese cooking for hundreds of years. It is believed that soy sauce was invented by accident – as a derivative of soybean sauce.

Traditionally, soybeans were first steamed then mixed with mould cultures like *Aspergillus oryzae* and wheat. After a few days the soybean mixture would be transferred to huge urns of brine and covered with a loose lid, and the mixture would ferment naturally under the sun for at least 6 months, allowing the soy sauce to reach its best natural flavour. During this long fermentation, the *Aspergillus oryzae* decomposes the soybean protein into amino acids, creating a special umami taste that's unique to soy sauce. The carbohydrates in the wheat also decompose into sugar, which makes the soy sauce fragrant and slightly sweet. Melanin and melanoids are produced during fermentation, which together make up the dark colour of soy sauce.

When choosing Chinese soy sauces at an Asian grocer, you will see that they are classified according to how much amino nitrogen they contain. The more amino nitrogen a soy sauce contains, the more umami it has and, therefore, it has a higher classification.

Grade	Amount amino nitrogen/ 100 ml (3½ fl oz)
Supreme	≥0.80 g (1/16 oz)
1	≥0.70 g (1/16 oz)
2	≥0.55 g (1/32 oz)
3	≥0.40 g (1/32 oz)

Nowadays, soy sauce production is carried out under strictly controlled conditions, and most of the soy sauces on the market aren't fermented for as long, with some as little as fifteen days.

LIGHT SOY SAUCE

(生抽) After an initial fermentation period, a portion of soy sauce is extracted. This is called the 'first extraction oil' (頭抽油). The remaining soy mixture is allowed to ferment until a second extraction is removed – the 'second extraction oil' (二抽油). It is left to ferment longer still, until the final 'third extraction oil' (三抽油) is removed.

Light soy sauce is made by mixing the first, second and third extraction oils in proportion – generally, the higher the percentage of the first extraction oil, the better quality the light soy sauce will be. Light soy sauce is much lighter in colour than dark soy sauce, but it has a saltier taste, and is normally used for stir-frying, cold dishes or dipping.

DARK SOY SAUCE

(老抽) Dark soy sauce is further processed and concentrated. Compared with light soy sauce, it has a much darker colour and greater viscosity, and is mostly used for colouring. Many brands add extra caramel colouring to their dark soy sauces to obtain an even darker colour and a slightly sweet taste.

CHINESE DARK VINEGAR

(**Chinkiang vinegar 鎮江香醋 / Baoning vinegar 保寧醋**) Besides soy sauce, dark vinegar is definitely one of the most important sauces in Chinese cooking. There are many different kinds of dark vinegars depending on the region, but the four most famous vinegars of China are Shanxi aged vinegar (山西老陳醋) from Shanxi, Chinkiang vinegar (鎮江香醋) from Jiangsu, Baoning vinegar (保寧醋) from Sichuan and Yongchun aged vinegar (永春老醋) from Fujian. The Shanxi aged vinegar is the most sour and has the strongest taste.

The one I use most often is the Chinkiang vinegar from the town of Zhenjiang in Jiangsu. It is especially good in cold dishes.

Its Chinese name, 香醋, means 'fragrant vinegar', as the vinegar has a very strong fragrance and is slightly sweet in taste. Chinkiang vinegar is made by first making rice wine with glutinous rice. Acetic acid bacteria is then added to the rice wine and allowed to brew over a long period of time.

Baoning vinegar is the other dark vinegar I use the most. This vinegar is from a small town called Baoning in Sichuan, and it has a history of over a thousand years. While Chinkiang vinegar uses only glutinous rice as its base, Baoning vinegar is made by combining bran, wheat, rice, corn, sorghum and buckwheat, and it is essential if you want to cook authentic Sichuan food.

RICE VINEGAR

(白米醋) Compared to Chinese dark vinegar that can be made with all kinds of grains, many rice vinegars have only two ingredients: rice and water. Rice vinegar is normally transparent, white or pale yellow in colour. A good rice vinegar isn't just sour; it also has a fragrant smell and mildly sweet taste, and is often used in sour spicy dishes.

VEGAN OYSTER SAUCE

(素蚝油/素蠔油) Oyster sauce is probably the most used sauce in modern Chinese cooking besides soy sauce. It was originally used in Cantonese cooking and has gradually become a very popular sauce all over China for its rich umami taste, which really enhances a dish's flavours. For vegetarians and vegans, there is a vegan oyster sauce you can find at almost every Asian grocer. It tastes similar to oyster sauce and is usually made from shiitake mushrooms.

Many sauces are called 'vegetarian sauce' but are actually vegan – but be sure to check. Vegan oyster sauces go by many names, depending on the brand and country the product is sold in, such as 'Vegetarian oyster-flavoured sauce' (素食蠔油),

'Vegetarian mushroom-flavoured stir-fry sauce' (素食蠔油), 'Vegetarian mushroom oyster sauce' (香菇素蠔油), etc. To avoid confusion in all these names, we use simply 'vegan oyster sauce' in the recipes to refer to this sauce.

PIXIAN BROAD BEAN PASTE

(郫縣豆瓣醬) Pixian broad bean paste is definitely the most fundamental condiment in Sichuan cooking. It is referred to as 'the soul of Sichuan food', and many Sichuan families make their own broad bean paste at home. Pixian is the name of a county which is now a part of Chengdu, and the climate there is ideal for the fermentation of broad bean paste. There are many different kinds of broad bean pastes in China, but just as only the Champagne produced in Champagne can be called by that name, only the broad bean paste that is produced in Pixian can be called 'Pixian broad bean paste'.

Pixian broad bean paste is bright red and has a salty, slightly spicy taste. As the name suggests, it is made with broad beans as well as Er jing tiao chillies, which are first fermented separately, then fermented together. Similar to soy sauce, broad bean paste was traditionally fermented for at least one year in large urns under the sun.

SESAME OIL

(芝麻油) Sesame oil is made from 100 per cent sesame. Most commercially available products are made from white sesame, but some are made from black sesame. Sometimes, other vegetable oils are added, so be sure to check the ingredients to make sure you are buying pure sesame oil.

Sesame oil is extremely fragrant, therefore it takes only a few drops to enhance the flavour of your dishes. It is normally used as a dressing for cold dishes or in dishes that don't require too much cooking, as the fragrance of the oil is reduced when heated.

If you would like to add sesame oil to a dish that needs long cooking, simply add it right at the end.

SESAME PASTE

(芝麻酱) Like sesame oil, sesame paste is also made from 100 per cent sesame, and only white sesame paste is used in common cooking. Chinese sesame paste is very fragrant and, like sesame oil, it is ideally used in cold dishes or in noodles, and it has a different taste and texture compared to tahini. Many sesame pastes in Asian grocers contain peanut butter or other nuts too, so always check the ingredients to make sure the product has been made exclusively with sesame.

Sesame paste can be quite dense, with a layer of oil floating on top of the almost solid paste. In this case the sesame paste must be diluted before use. Many people would simply mix the sesame paste with hot water to make a liquid, but this reduces the paste's fragrance. The best method is to mix the sesame paste with some sesame oil, stirring until it becomes smoother and the fragrance is well preserved.

FIVE SPICE

(五香) Five spice is one of the most classic Chinese spice blends. It normally consists of cinnamon, star anise, sichuan peppercorn, fennel seed and clove, but sometimes other spices are also added. Five spice is normally sold in the form of ground powder. The mix is very aromatic and a little bit goes a long way. It is used very commonly in the making of master stock and barbecue.

THIRTEEN SPICE

(十三香) Thirteen spice is another common Chinese spice blend that is also sold as a ground powder. It normally consists of orange peel, cinnamon, cumin, white cardamom, bay leaf, sichuan peppercorn, star anise, nutmeg, galangal, chilli, clove, licorice and tsaoko. This spice blend has a more complex and strong flavour than five spice.

PREPARATION TIME
5 minutes

COOKING TIME
20 minutes

MAKES
500 ml (17 fl oz/2 cups)

This is a typical chilli oil recipe from Sichuan. The oil is first heated with many different spices in it and then poured over the chilli flakes. You can use canola oil or corn oil for this, but avoid using oils with a low smoking point, like olive oil.

The finished oil is very aromatic and rich in taste, and it makes the perfect base seasoning for many recipes, especially cold dishes like noodles and salads.

油泼辣子

CHILLI OIL

100 g (3½ oz) chilli flakes

30 g (1 oz) toasted white sesame seeds

50 g (1¾ oz) piece of fresh ginger, peeled

1 cinnamon stick

3 star anise

1 tsaoko pod

5 dried bay leaves

1 tablespoon cloves

1 tablespoon sichuan peppercorns

5 g (⅛ oz) sand ginger

500 ml (17 fl oz/2 cups) vegetable oil

50 g (1¾ oz) leek stem, cut into large chunks

½ teaspoon thirteen spice

In a large bowl, combine the chilli flakes and sesame and set aside.

Smack the ginger a bit with the flat edge of a knife to crush it a little, then slice it. Rinse all the dried whole spices – leaving out the thirteen spice – quickly under water so they don't burn when cooked.

Add the oil to a saucepan set over a medium–low heat. Add the ginger and leek, cinnamon stick, star anise, tsaoko and sand ginger and fry for about 10 minutes. Add the bay leaves and fry for 2 minutes before adding the cloves and sichuan peppercorns, stirring for another 3 minutes. When the oil reaches 160–170°C (320–340°F) – you can tell it's hot enough when lots of tiny bubbles immediately form around a wooden chopstick placed into the oil – carefully strain the hot oil through a fine-mesh sieve into a clean saucepan or jug. Pour half of the oil slowly over the chilli flakes and sesame. Stir to mix well, then wait 30 seconds before pouring in the rest of the hot oil. Stir again, then add the thirteen spice and mix well.

Allow to cool completely before pouring into a clean bottle or similar airtight container. The oil will keep for months stored in a cool, dark place. Just make sure you use a clean spoon every time to avoid contaminating the oil.

PREPARATION TIME
3 hours

COOKING TIME
20 minutes

MAKES
approx. 600 g (1 lb 5 oz)

Traditionally, pickling was the most common way to preserve vegetables, especially prior to industrial farming which allowed vegetables to be grown year-round. Different cuisines employ different pickling methods, and in China, the methods differ between regions too. The method I used here is commonly used in Sichuan, and with this formula you can basically pickle any veggie you want, such as radish, chilli, cabbage or long green beans.

巷碟泡菜

BASIC PICKLE

1 kg (2 lb 3 oz) vegetables of your choice

180 g (6½ oz) salt

15 g (½ oz) sichuan peppercorns

3 litres (101 fl oz/12 cups) boiled water

100–150 ml (3½–5 fl oz) liquor (I use rice wine with 35% alcohol, or vodka or gin – anything 30% or higher)

Wash the vegetables, removing any dirt or excess leaves or stalks, and trim to fit a jar – or jars, as needed. Put the vegetables somewhere warm and dry to allow the water on the surface to completely evaporate – this can take a few hours. It's very important to make sure the vegetables are completely dry before you begin.

Rinse your jars with boiling water, then set aside to dry.

Combine the salt and sichuan peppercorns in a large clean bowl. Add the just-boiled water and stir a little to dissolve the salt. Alternatively, you can wait until the water cools down to add the salt and peppercorns, but this will result in a lighter brine and will take longer for the salt to dissolve.

Pack the vegetables into the jars and add enough brine to cover the vegetables but still leave a 3 cm (1¼ in) gap between the brine and the opening of the jar. Add 50 ml (1¾ fl oz) liquor to each jar, then seal tightly and store somewhere nice and dry away from direct sunlight.

The pickle should be ready in about 3 weeks in winter, 1 week in summer. Make sure you use a clean, dry utensil each time to remove the vegetables to avoid contamination.

TIPS: It is very important to make sure that no water (besides the boiled water for the brine) gets on anything that comes in direct contact with the veggies. Also, after washing the veggies, make sure they are thoroughly dry before pickling to avoid any mould forming during fermentation.

After 3–5 days of fermentation gases start to accumulate inside the jar. It's recommended that you open the lid of the jar every 3–5 days for a second just to release the gases.

If you take some of the pickled veggies out, you can put some fresh ones in. Just make sure there is no water on the surface and top up with salted water accordingly – boil some water, add salt and wait for it to cool before adding to the jar. The amount of salt should be 6 per cent of the weight of the water.

PREPARATION TIME
5 minutes

COOKING TIME
15 minutes

MAKES
300 ml (10 fl oz)

Red soy sauce is a basic condiment that is widely used in Sichuan cooking, especially in cold dishes and noodles, for example in xiao mian, Tianshui noodles and Sichuan cold noodles. Essentially, soy sauce is simmered with spices to create a thicker, more aromatic and multi-layered flavour.

複合醬油

RED SOY SAUCE

350 ml (12 fl oz) soy sauce

80 g (2¾ oz/⅓ cup) brown sugar

70 g (2½ oz) crystal sugar

30 g (1 oz) piece of fresh ginger, sliced

5 g (⅛ oz) sand ginger

5 coriander (cilantro) sprigs with roots

4 spring onions (scallions)

6 dried bay leaves

6 star anise

1 cinnamon stick

1 tsaoko pod

1 teaspoon cumin seeds

1 teaspoon cloves

Add the soy sauce to a large saucepan with 90 ml (3 fl oz) water and place over a medium heat. Add the brown sugar and stir until it's dissolved.

Add the remaining ingredients to the pot and stir a little. When it starts to boil, reduce the heat to low and let the sauce simmer for about 15 minutes until it has reduced by one-third. Remove from the heat.

Once cool, strain the aromatics out of the sauce and store the sauce in an airtight container in the fridge for up to 3 months.

Tianmian sauce is commonly used in northern China. Although it's also called 'sweet bean sauce' or 'sweet bean paste', it is mainly made with fermented wheat flour. It is a staple ingredient in many northern Chinese dishes, for example in zhajiang noodles and as the dipping sauce for Peking duck. This tianmian sauce can be prepared within minutes and requires very few ingredients.

PREPARATION TIME
5 minutes

COOKING TIME
15 minutes

MAKES
250 g (9 oz)

甜麵醬

TIANMIAN (SWEET BEAN) SAUCE

Mix all the ingredients, except the oil, in a bowl with 250 ml (8½ fl oz/ 1 cup) water. Stir well, ensuring there are no lumps in the sauce.

Heat a saucepan over a medium–low heat. Once hot, add the oil and the sauce.

Stir for a few minutes until the sauce has thickened, then turn off the heat. Once cool, store the sauce in an airtight container in the fridge for up to 1 month.

3 tablespoons soy sauce

2 tablespoons vegan oyster sauce

1 tablespoon dark soy sauce

30 g (1 oz) sugar

20 g (¾ oz) plain (all-purpose) flour

2 tablespoons canola (rapeseed) oil

PREPARATION TIME
20 minutes

COOKING TIME
20 minutes

MAKES
800 ml (27 fl oz)

Laoganma is the most famous sauce brand in China and is definitely one of the bestsellers worldwide. There are many sauces and condiments from Laoganma, but their staple product has always been the classic preserved black beans with chilli (風味豆豉油製辣椒). This sauce essentially goes with everything. You can use it in cooking, to dress cold dishes or salads, or to top noodles and rice. The ingredients are fairly simple – you really only need dried chilli and fermented black beans.

自製老乾媽

HOME-MADE LAOGANMA SAUCE

200 g (7 oz) dried chillies
100 g (3½ oz) fermented black beans
500 ml (17 fl oz/2 cups) vegetable oil
2 tablespoons sugar
salt, to taste

Soak the dried chilli in hot water for 10 minutes, then drain and blend the chilli for 1 minute in a high-speed blender. Steam the fermented black beans for 15 minutes.

Place the wok over a high heat for 30 seconds then add the oil. When the oil is hot, switch the heat to medium–low and add the chilli. Fry the chilli slowly until it is not soggy anymore, about 10–15 minutes.

Add the black beans, stirring for about 5 minutes until the whole sauce is very aromatic. Turn off the heat and add the sugar and salt to taste. Once cool, store in an airtight container in the fridge for at least 3 months.

PREPARATION TIME
15 minutes

COOKING TIME
10 minutes

MAKES
600 ml (20½ fl oz)

This chilli sauce with garlic has a really zingy kick. It is ideal for barbecued foods, cold dishes and many noodle dishes.

蒜蓉辣椒醬

CHILLI SAUCE WITH GARLIC

90 ml (3 fl oz) canola (rapeseed) oil

3 garlic heads, cloves peeled and finely chopped

20 g (¾ oz) piece of fresh ginger, peeled and finely chopped

200 g (7 oz) fresh red chilli, destemmed and finely chopped

1 teaspoon salt

1 teaspoon sugar

1 tablespoon vegan oyster sauce

Heat a wok over a medium heat and add the oil. When the oil is hot, add the garlic and ginger and stir for 2–3 minutes.

Add the chopped chilli and stir for another 2–3 minutes before adding the salt, sugar and vegan oyster sauce. Stir for another minute, then turn off the heat and allow the sauce to cool. Store in an airtight container in the fridge for up to 1 month.

This chopped chilli sauce is very traditional in Hunan – almost every family makes their own, as spicy is the fundamental element of Hunanese cuisine. It's also a good way to preserve chilli. In the past, many Hunanese dishes that were made with fresh chilli when it was in season were made using this chilli sauce or dried chilli during other seasons.

Normally, small and very spicy chillies are used, like the facing heaven chilli or bird's eye chilli, but you can also use less spicy varieties. The only thing to watch out for is – just like pickling other vegetables – there is absolutely no water or oil on the ingredients or anything that comes in contact with them (the knife, cutting board or container), otherwise your pickle could be mouldy within a few days.

PREPARATION TIME
1 hour

MAKES
150 g (5½ oz)

剁辣椒

PICKLED CHOPPED CHILLI

Wash the chillies and put them somewhere dry for a few hours until there is no water left on the surface, then chop.

Mix the chopped chilli with the garlic, salt and liquor, and put it in an airtight container. Store in the fridge for at least 6 months. Make sure to use a clean spoon to take it out every time to avoid contamination.

200 g (7 oz) fresh red chillies, destemmed

3 garlic cloves, finely chopped

20 g (¾ oz) salt

3 tablespoons 30% liquor, such as rice liquor

PREPARATION TIME
5 minutes

COOKING TIME
15 minutes

MAKES
250 ml (8½ fl oz/1 cup)

Char siu sauce is a sweet and savoury sauce typically used to marinate and make char siu, the Cantonese-style barbecued pork. But the sauce is versatile for marinating and cooking.

叉燒汁

CHAR SIU SAUCE

90 ml (3 fl oz) soy sauce

1 tablespoon dark soy sauce

90 ml (3 fl oz) vegan oyster sauce

120 g (4½ oz) sugar

2 tablespoons Chinese cooking wine

1 tablespoon cornflour (cornstarch)

60 ml (2 fl oz/¼ cup) canola (rapeseed) oil

6 garlic cloves, finely chopped

½ onion, finely chopped

Mix all the ingredients, except for the oil, garlic and onion, in a bowl with 90 ml (3 fl oz) water.

Heat a wok over a medium heat. Once hot, add the oil, garlic and onion and stir for 1–2 minutes until the garlic and onion turn a bit brown.

Add the sauce and reduce the heat to medium–low. Keep stirring for a few minutes until the sauce has thickened, then turn off the heat. After the sauce has cooled down, store in an airtight container in the fridge for up to 1 month.

There are many versions of hot pot in China, but the most well known one is, for sure, the spicy hot pot from Sichuan and Chongqing. In Chengdu, many hot pot restaurants are open 24/7, so you can imagine how popular hot pot is there. It is the kind of food I crave more when the weather gets colder. The beauty of hot pot is that you can cook literally anything you like in it. That's why hot pot is the go-to food choice for gatherings with friends and family, as it brings people together and makes everyone happy.

This hot pot paste is not difficult to make at home if you can source the ingredients. You can store it in the fridge for a week or in the freezer for up to 3 months.

When preparing a hot pot, simply add water to the hot pot paste at a ratio of one-part water to three-parts paste. When the hot pot soup starts to boil, add your ingredients, starting with the ones that will take the longest to cook (see the tip for some suggestions).

PREPARATION TIME
1 hour

COOKING TIME
1 hour

MAKES
2.5 kg (5½ lb)

火鍋底料

HOT POT PASTE

Soak the cinnamon, star anise, tsaoko, fennel seeds, white cardamom, cloves, sand ginger powder, licorice and wurfbainia villosa in water for 30 minutes. Soak 300 g (10½ oz) of the dried chillies in water for 20 minutes.

Drain the water from the spices, then put the spices in a blender and blend for 15 seconds so they are a bit smaller, but not too fine. Drain the chilli then chop or blend finely. Finely chop the fermented black beans.

Soak the remaining dried chillies with the bay leaves in warm water for 10 minutes, then drain.

Add the sichuan peppercorns to a bowl with the liquor.

Heat a wok, then add the oil. When the oil is beginning to warm, add the garlic, the sliced ginger, leek and coriander and fry until golden, about 10–15 minutes, over a medium–low heat so they don't burn. Remove the ingredients from the oil and discard.

Add the chopped dried chilli to the oil and turn the heat down to low. Fry, stirring continuously, for 10–15 minutes.

3 cinnamon sticks	
15 g (½ oz) star anise	
2 tsaoko pods	
10 g (¼ oz) fennel seeds	
10 g (¼ oz) white cardamom pods, bruised	
10 g (¼ oz) cloves	
20 g (¾ oz) sand ginger	
5 g (⅛ oz) licorice, dried and sliced	
10 g (¼ oz) wurfbainia villosa	
350 g (12½ oz) dried chillies	
20 g (¾ oz) fermented black beans	
10 g (¼ oz) dried bay leaves	

20 g (¾ oz) green sichuan peppercorns

2 tablespoons 30% liquor, such as rice liquor

1.5 litres (51 fl oz/6 cups) canola (rapeseed) oil

10 garlic cloves, peeled

120 g (4½ oz) piece of fresh ginger, peeled, 100 g (3½ oz) sliced and 20 g (¾ oz) finely chopped

250 g (9 oz) leek, cut into big chunks

100 g (3½ oz) coriander (cilantro) sprigs

600 g (1 lb 5 oz) Pixian broad bean paste (see page 26)

50 g (1¾ oz) crystal sugar

200 ml (7 fl oz) sweet rice wine

Drain the chilli and bay leaves and add them to the oil. Fry for 1 minute, then add the Pixian broad bean paste. Fry for about 15–20 minutes, stirring occasionally.

Add the fermented black beans and the chopped ginger and fry for another 5 minutes. Add the drained spices from step one and fry for 15 minutes.

Add the green sichuan peppercorns with the wine and fry for 5 minutes before adding the crystal sugar and sweet rice wine. Cook for another 5–10 minutes, then turn off the heat. It is better to let the hot pot soup base sit for 12–24 hours at room temperature (or in the fridge if it's summer) before eating so that all the flavours can blend together.

TIP: I usually prepare hot pot with king oyster, oyster, shiitake or enoki mushrooms, tofu, tofu puffs, yuba, pak choi, Shirataki noodle knots and sweet potato noodles. I start with the ingredients that take the longest to cook, such as the mushrooms and tofu puffs. Anything that cooks very quickly (like leafy green vegetables) should be added last and only cooked about 30 seconds. Usually, I serve hot pot with dips made from sesame oil, garlic, red chilli, sesame paste, spring onion (scallion) and coriander (cilantro).

PREPARATION TIME
15 minutes

COOKING TIME
15 minutes

MAKES
300 ml (10 fl oz)

Golden and silver garlic sauce is used mostly in Cantonese cooking, usually to steam or grill seafood. It is extremely fragrant and enhances the flavour of basically anything you add it to. It is called 'golden and silver garlic' because 30 per cent of the garlic is fried until golden on the outside, 50 per cent is fried until very fragrant but not coloured, and the other 20 per cent is added raw.

金銀蒜

GOLDEN AND SILVER GARLIC SAUCE

200 g (7 oz) garlic, chopped

240 ml (8 fl oz) canola (rapeseed) oil

20 g (¾ oz) piece of fresh ginger, peeled and chopped

1 tablespoon vegan oyster sauce

1 tablespoon soy sauce

1 teaspoon sugar

1 teaspoon salt

Rinse the garlic under running water for 1 minute – to help get rid of the bitterness after frying – then separate the garlic into three portions at a ratio of 3:5:2.

Heat a wok over a medium–low heat, then add the oil. Add 30 per cent of all the garlic and allow to fry until it's golden on the outside. Use a small sieve to take it out and set aside.

Switch to the lowest heat and add 50 per cent of all the garlic and the ginger. Stir for 1–2 minutes, then add the vegan oyster sauce, soy sauce, sugar and salt. Turn off the heat and add the raw garlic along with the reserved fried garlic. Once cool, store in an airtight container in the fridge for up to 1 month.

Sesame paste is different from tahini and is used in many Chinese dishes. If you are not able to find Chinese sesame paste where you live, it is very easy to make yourself – it only takes three ingredients and 10 minutes.

芝麻醬

SESAME PASTE/ SAUCE

200 g (7 oz) white sesame seeds

3 tablespoons sesame oil

½ teaspoon salt

Heat a non-stick frying pan over a medium–low heat and, when hot, add the sesame seeds and stir and toast for a few minutes until they are slightly brown and very aromatic.

Remove to a high-speed blender and add the sesame oil and salt. Blend to a smooth sauce.

The sesame paste can be kept in an airtight jar for at least 3 months at room temperature, or longer if stored in the fridge.

ALL ABOUT TOFU

The history of tofu dates back more than two thousand years in China. Tofu has played an essential role in the Chinese diet and was, for a very long time, the main source of protein for most people. To make most kinds of tofu you only need soybeans. The difference between varieties of tofu mainly depends on which coagulant is used and how hard and long the tofu is pressed. In general, the longer the tofu is pressed, the less water it contains and the firmer it becomes.

Most people are only familiar with the common firm tofu that is sold in supermarkets, and many struggle to cook with it. But, just like cheese, tofu is extremely diverse and versatile; there are more than a hundred kinds of tofu in China alone and even more ways to prepare it, and Hunan is one of the regions with the largest variety of tofu.

Given it holds such a significant place in the Chinese diet, and in the vegan diet more generally, I would like to give a brief introduction to some of the most common kinds of tofu and soybean products here.

Apart from the vacuum-packed tofu you can find at most supermarkets, at many bigger Asian grocers you will also be able to find fresh tofu that is made locally and delivered to the store right after production. At every market in China you'll find a tofu stand selling freshly made tofu products, and this is my favourite kind of tofu to buy, but the downside of fresh tofu is that it should be consumed as soon as possible (ideally on the day you buy it, and certainly no longer than 48 hours afterwards), otherwise it can go sour quickly, especially when the weather is hot. The best way to store tofu is to put it in a lunchbox and immerse it completely in clean water before storing in the fridge.

If you would like to experience the fun of making your own tofu at home, you would need soybeans, nigari salt or edible gypsum powder, and a tofu press which you can find at some Asian stores or online. If you don't have the time or resources, feel free to just jump ahead and buy some tofu at your local store for the recipes in this tofu chapter.

TENDER TOFU

(嫩豆腐) Tender tofu is firmer than silken tofu but more tender and easily breakable than firm tofu. It is my preferred tofu for cooking due to its smooth texture and mild taste. Edible gypsum powder is normally used as the coagulant for tender tofu.

After deep-frying or pan-frying, tender tofu becomes golden and crispy on the outside and succulent on the inside. Frying gives tofu a special taste and texture, and with a bit of salt sprinkled on it, it can be a delicious and easy snack by itself. When it is cooked again with other sauces, it absorbs the flavours and becomes extremely juicy and tasty.

FIRM TOFU

(老豆腐/北豆腐) Firm tofu contains less water than tender tofu and therefore is firmer and less breakable. Instead of edible gypsum powder, nigari salt is normally used as the coagulant. Firm tofu is used more often in stir-fries, where the ingredients need to be stirred constantly, as it holds its shape better. When cooked in a sauce or stew, it will not be as juicy and succulent as tender tofu.

FRESH TOFU SKIN/PRESSED TOFU SHEETS

(豆腐皮/千張) This product has a lot of names in both Chinese and English. Where I'm from we call it '豆腐皮', which translates directly as 'tofu skin', but 'tofu skin' is also used to refer to dried tofu sheets. The tofu skin we are talking about here is the freshly pressed tofu sheets. The tofu is pressed extra hard and long to obtain the firm and durable consistency, which is quite elastic and slightly chewy. Fresh tofu skin is often used in cold dishes, salads, braised dishes, hot pot and barbecue.

TOFU STICKS/YUBA

(腐竹) Tofu sticks are made from the thin layer of skin that forms on the surface of simmering soy milk. The milk skin is removed, squeezed together and hung until it's dry.

The first step to preparing tofu sticks is to soak them for 2 hours in room-temperature water. Avoid using hot water, otherwise the outside of the tofu sticks will break while the inside will remain hard. They are used often in cold dishes such as cucumber salad, stewed dishes, stir-fries, soups and hot pot.

FUPI/DRIED TOFU SHEETS

(腐皮/油豆皮) Fupi is essentially made the same way as tofu sticks, only when the soy milk skin is formed, it is carefully removed with a long stick to maintain its flat shape, then it's hung until dried. Fupi is often used to wrap other ingredients before the wrap is steamed or deep-fried. For example, there is a famous Cantonese dim sum called 'fupi rolls'. It is also used in cold dishes, soups and hot pot.

There are two kinds of fupi you can normally find at an Asian grocer: one is soft and the other is hard and crispy. The soft one can be used directly to wrap foods, but the hard one should be soaked for a few minutes until it softens before use. Hard fupi can also be cut into small pieces and deep-fried to use as a noodle topping or in hot pot.

TOFU PUFFS

(油豆腐/豆泡) Tofu puffs are deep-fried tofu. To make the fluffiest tofu puffs, the most important thing is to have exactly the right kind of fresh firm tofu, made with nigari salt as the coagulant, which makes it difficult to make tofu puffs from scratch at home, but you will be able to find them at many Asian grocers. Fresh tofu puffs should be consumed within three days, otherwise they should be stored in the freezer.

Tofu puffs are very soft and fluffy compared to other kinds of fried tofu. The porous texture makes them the perfect ingredient for any dish with a sauce, as the puffs will absorb a lot of the sauce during cooking and become very juicy and flavourful.

SMOKED TOFU

(香干) To make smoked tofu you must first make semi-firm or firm tofu, braise the tofu in a sauce seasoned with spices, then smoke it and allow the tofu to air-dry for a bit. There are dozens of different kinds of smoked tofu just in Hunan alone, so it can be easily found in many Hunanese dishes. It has a unique smoky flavour and chewy texture, and it is used mostly in quick stir-fries.

PREPARATION TIME
6 hours

COOKING TIME
10 minutes

SERVES
4

As well as being the main ingredient in tofu, soy milk also is the most popular breakfast drink in China. You can soak the soybeans the night before and make it in the morning for breakfast. It's hearty but fresh. You can drink it hot or cold, plain or with sugar. For drinking, the ratio of soybeans to water should be 1:10. If you plan to make soy milk for tofu or tofu pudding, then the ratio of soybeans to water should be 1:8 (e.g. 100 g/3½ oz soybeans to 800 ml/27 fl oz water).

豆漿

SOY MILK

150 g (5½ oz) dried soybeans

Soak the soybeans in water for at least 6 hours, or overnight.

Drain the water, add the soaked soybeans to a soy milk machine or blender and add 1.5 litres (51 fl oz/6 cups) water.

If you use a soy milk machine, choose the soy milk program. If you use a high-speed blender, blend for 2 minutes.

Line a sieve set over a pan or bowl with a thin cotton cloth or muslin (cheesecloth) to filter the soy milk. Pour in the milk, then squeeze the soy bulb in the cotton cloth to get the remaining soy milk out.

Heat the soy milk in a large saucepan over a medium heat. Just before the milk comes to the boil, some foam will accumulate on the surface. Reduce the heat to the lowest setting and skim the foam with a small sieve or slotted spoon and discard. Increase the heat and allow the milk to boil for 2–3 minutes, then turn off the heat. Cool and store in the fridge for up to 48 hours.

To make tofu from scratch, first you need fresh soy milk. In the previous recipe I have shared how to make fresh soy milk with soybeans. If the soy milk is used for making tofu, the ratio should be 1:8, which means for 100 g (3½ oz) dried soybeans, after they are soaked, 800 ml (27 fl oz) water should be added to the blender with the soybeans.

Normally, tender tofu should be formed after pressing for 30 minutes, but if you want it to be slightly firmer and contain less water, you can press it for 10–20 minutes longer.

The one special piece of equipment you need for making tofu is a tofu mould, which you should be able to find at most big Asian stores or online shops.

You can use tender tofu for all kinds of dishes, such as Mapo tofu (page 61), Pan-fried tofu with fresh green chilli (page 71) and Spring onion tofu (page 75), or you can even eat it raw.

PREPARATION TIME
1 hour

COOKING TIME
10 minutes

SERVES
2

自製嫩豆腐
TENDER TOFU

Half-fill a large stockpot with water and bring to the boil. Once the water is boiling, cover the pot with a lid and turn off the heat. Select a heatproof bowl big enough to hold the soy milk and that will fit inside the stockpot containing the water.

Mix the gypsum powder with 2 tablespoons water, stirring until it is completely dissolved, then add it to the bowl. Place the bowl in the stockpot of water, but be careful that no water gets inside the bowl.

Bring the soy milk to the boil in a large saucepan over a medium heat. Just before the milk boils, some foam will accumulate on the surface. Reduce the heat to the lowest setting and skim the foam with a small sieve or slotted spoon and discard. Increase the heat and allow the milk to boil for 2–3 minutes, then turn off the heat and set it aside for 2 minutes.

Mix the gypsum water again quickly and carefully pour the soy milk into the bowl inside the stockpot. Stir gently for 5–10 seconds, then cover the pot with a lid and let the soy milk rest for 30 minutes. Make sure there is enough hot water in the pot to keep the soy milk warm the whole time; if the temperature is too low, the coagulation won't be successful.

7 g (¼ oz) edible gypsum powder

2 litres (68 fl oz/8 cups) Soy milk (page 55), uncooked

After 30 minutes of resting, the tofu pudding should be done. Place a thin cotton cloth or muslin (cheesecloth) in the tofu mould then add the tofu pudding. Cover the top with the cloth so the tofu is completely wrapped by the cloth. Put the lid on the mould and weigh it down with something heavy on top (like a pot of water). Leave it for 30 minutes.

After 30 minutes the tofu should be compressed. Carefully remove the cloth from the tofu. If you're not planning to use it immediately, it can be stored in the fridge. Place it in an airtight container and add enough water to submerge the tofu. Cover with the lid and refrigerate for up to 48 hours.

Firm tofu contains less water than tender tofu, and instead of edible gypsum powder, nigari salt is normally used as the coagulant. The consistency of firm tofu is elastic and a little rough compared to the easily breakable and smooth tender tofu. Firm tofu is good for soups, stews, barbecues or cooking in a Chinese master stock. It is also the right tofu to use when making smoked tofu.

You will need a tofu mould for this recipe, which you should be able to find at most big Asian stores or online shops.

老豆腐/北豆腐
FIRM TOFU

PREPARATION TIME
1 hour 15 minutes

COOKING TIME
10 minutes

SERVES
2

Half-fill a large stockpot with water and bring to the boil. Once the water is boiling, cover the pot with a lid and turn off the heat. Select a heatproof bowl big enough to hold the soy milk and that will fit inside the saucepan containing the water.

Mix the nigari salt with 2 tablespoons water, stirring until it's completely dissolved. Add it to the bowl. Place the bowl in the stockpot of water, but be careful that no water gets inside the bowl.

Bring the soy milk to the boil in a large saucepan over a medium heat. Just before the milk boils, some foam will accumulate on the surface. Reduce the heat to the lowest setting and skim the foam with a small sieve or slotted spoon and discard. Increase the heat and allow the milk to boil for 2–3 minutes, then turn off the heat and set it aside for 2 minutes.

Pour the soy milk into the bowl inside the pot that contains the nigari water. Stir gently for 5–10 seconds, then cover the pot with a lid and let the soy milk rest in the warm water for 30 minutes. Make sure there is enough hot water in the pot to keep the soy milk warm the whole time. If the temperature is too low, the coagulation won't be successful.

After 30 minutes of resting, the tofu pudding should be done. Place a thin cotton cloth or muslin (cheesecloth) on the tofu mould then add the tofu. Cover the top with the cloth so the tofu is completely wrapped by the cloth. Put the lid on the mould and weigh it down with something heavy on top (like a pot of water). Leave it for 30–40 minutes; the longer it is pressed, the firmer the tofu will be.

7 g (¼ oz) nigari salt

2 litres (68 fl oz/8 cups) Soy milk (page 55), uncooked

After 30–40 minutes the tofu should be compressed. Carefully remove the cloth from the tofu. If you're not planning to use it immediately, it can be stored in the fridge. Place it in an airtight container and add enough water to submerge the tofu. Cover with the lid and refrigerate for up to 48 hours.

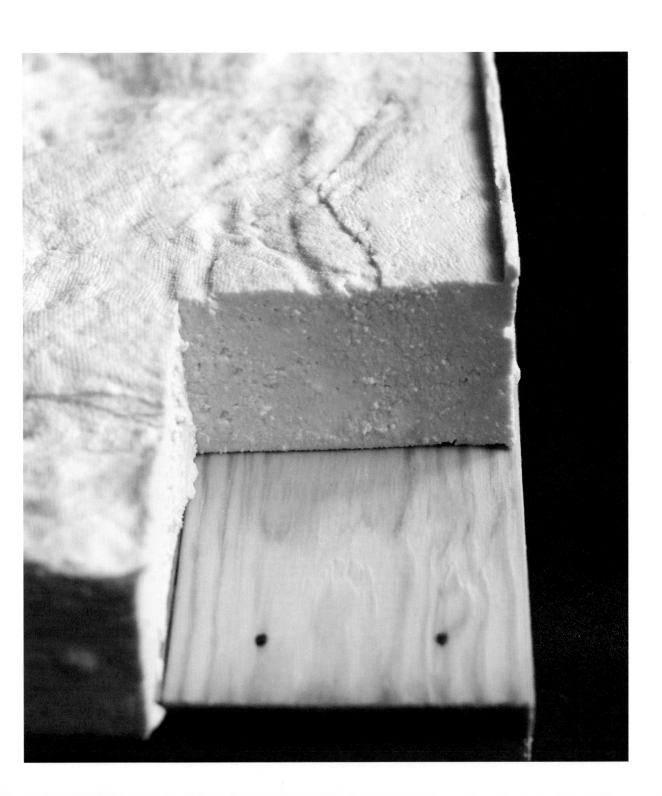

PREPARATION TIME
15 minutes

COOKING TIME
15 minutes

SERVES
2

Mapo tofu is one of the most loved tofu dishes ever, and is certainly a signature dish of Sichuan cuisine. Mapo (麻婆) means 'an older woman with a freckled face' in Chinese. Allegedly, the dish was invented by a woman who ran a small restaurant in Chengdu, Sichuan, in 1862. She was called Mapo because of the freckles on her face.

Mapo tofu is known to be mouth-numbing, spicy, tender and aromatic. It is traditionally cooked with minced (ground) beef, but in this recipe I substitute it with a vegan mince, which also provides a very good taste.

麻婆豆腐

MAPO TOFU

750 g (1 lb 11 oz) tender tofu, cut into 2 cm (¾ in) dice

60 ml (2 fl oz/¼ cup) canola (rapeseed) oil

100 g (3½ oz) vegan mince

100 g (3½ oz) Pixian broad bean paste (see page 26)

60 ml (2 fl oz/¼ cup) Chilli oil (page 29)

1 tablespoon chilli flakes

1 tablespoon fermented black beans

3 garlic cloves, finely chopped

360 ml (12 fl oz) hot water

1 tablespoon soy sauce

1 tablespoon cornflour (cornstarch)

90 ml (3 fl oz) warm water

½ teaspoon ground sichuan peppercorns

1 green garlic stalk, cut into short lengths

Bring a saucepan of water to the boil on a medium heat and add the tofu. Boil for 1 minute, then remove from the water and set aside.

Heat a wok over a medium heat. Once hot, add 3 tablespoons of the oil and the vegan mince, breaking it into small pieces with a spatula. Stir-fry for a few minutes until the mince is slightly crispy and brown on the outside, then remove from the heat and set it aside for later.

Add the remaining oil to the wok and fry the Pixian broad bean paste for about 1 minute, then add the chilli oil, chilli flakes and fermented black beans. Stir a little, then add the garlic and stir for 30 seconds. Carefully add the tofu, then pour in the hot water and soy sauce.

When the sauce starts simmering, mix the cornflour with the warm water and add half of the cornflour water. Stir carefully and let it come to a simmer again.

When the sauce has reduced by half, turn the heat down to medium-low and add half of the remaining starchy water. Stir and let it simmer for a few minutes until the sauce has thickened, then add the rest of the starchy water. Let it simmer for another minute, stir gently so the tofu doesn't stick to the wok, then turn off the heat.

Carefully transfer the tofu to a bowl and top with the ground sichuan peppercorns and the green garlic.

Home-style tofu was originally a popular home dish from Sichuan, hence the name. For this dish, triangle-shaped tofu is first pan-fried then braised in a sauce. After cooking in the sauce, the tofu is juicy, savoury and slightly spicy.

PREPARATION TIME
30 minutes

COOKING TIME
15 minutes

SERVES
2

家常豆腐

HOME-STYLE TOFU

Soak the wood ear mushrooms for 20 minutes in water, then drain. Boil them for 1 minute, then drain and slice them.

Slice the tofu into pieces of about 5 mm (¼ in) thick, then cut them diagonally into triangles.

Heat a wok over a high heat and, once hot, add 60 ml (2 fl oz/¼ cup) of the oil. Pan-fry the tofu slices until both sides are golden and crispy, then take them out.

Reduce the heat to medium and add the remaining oil along with the garlic and ginger. Stir for 15 seconds then add the onion and carrot and stir-fry for 1 minute. Add the wood ear mushrooms and stir for 30 seconds.

Add the Pixian broad bean paste and keep stirring for 1 minute until it's well combined with the other ingredients. Add the tofu, soy sauce and vegan oyster sauce, mixing everything together well. Add the veggie stock or hot water and cook for about 5 minutes, stirring occasionally.

When half of the sauce has been absorbed by the tofu, mix the cornflour with 2 tablespoons water and pour it in. Add the green capsicum and mix it into the sauce. When most of the sauce is gone, stir through the green garlic and remove from the heat.

5 g (⅛ oz) wood ear mushrooms

500 g (1 lb 2 oz) tender or firm tofu

90 ml (3 fl oz) canola (rapeseed) oil

3 garlic cloves, finely sliced

10 g (¼ oz) piece of fresh ginger, peeled and finely chopped

½ onion, sliced

50 g (1¾ oz) carrot, sliced

20 g (¾ oz) Pixian broad bean paste (see page 26)

1 tablespoon soy sauce

1 tablespoon vegan oyster sauce

120 ml (4 fl oz) vegetable stock or hot water

1 teaspoon cornflour (cornstarch)

1 green capsicum (bell pepper), cut into short lengths

1 green garlic stalk or spring onion (scallion), cut into short lengths

The clay pot is a beloved piece of cooking equipment in China. It heats up more evenly and preserves heat much longer than metal pots, therefore it's ideal for stewed dishes that need to be cooked slowly. And it's believed that a clay pot can better preserve the healthy phenolic substances and original flavours of ingredients too.

For this recipe, the tofu is first deep-fried then sliced and cooked in the clay pot with the sauce and other ingredients. It's savoury, juicy and slightly spicy.

砂鍋豆腐

CLAY POT TOFU

90 ml (3 fl oz) canola (rapeseed) oil

500 g (1 lb 2 oz) tender or firm tofu, cut into 5 mm (¼ in) slices

½ onion, sliced

3 garlic cloves, sliced

10 g (¼ oz) piece of fresh ginger, cut into strips

5 bird's eye chillies, destemmed and sliced

2 tablespoons soy sauce

2 tablespoons vegan oyster sauce

75 ml (2½ fl oz) vegetable stock or water

1 teaspoon cornflour (cornstarch)

100 g (3½ oz) garlic scapes, cut into short lengths

1 spring onion (scallion), cut into short lengths

Heat a wok over a medium–high heat and add half of the oil. Pan-fry the tofu until it's golden and crispy on both sides, then set aside. Put the onion into a clay pot.

Add the remaining oil to the wok and add the garlic and ginger. Stir for 30 seconds, then add the chilli and stir for 15 seconds.

In a bowl, mix the soy sauce, vegan oyster sauce, vegetable stock and cornflour. Add the tofu to the sauce, mix well, and pour everything into the clay pot.

Add the garlic scapes to the clay pot, put the lid on and simmer over a medium–low heat for about 10 minutes until most of the sauce has reduced. Add the spring onion and serve.

Fried tofu is very crispy on the outside and extremely tender and juicy on the inside. It works well in many different dishes (such as Fried tofu puffs with green chilli and garlic scapes, page 81), but it is so easy and quick to make that you can just sprinkle it with salt and eat it as a snack. You can also dip it in almost anything you like – my favourite dipping sauce is a preserved plum sauce.

炸豆腐
FRIED TOFU

360 ml (12 fl oz) canola (rapeseed) oil

500 g (1 lb 2 oz) tender or firm tofu, cut into 2 cm (¾ in) dice

1 spring onion (scallion), finely sliced, to serve

Add the oil to a frying pan and heat it over a high heat. Once hot, add the tofu, being careful not to make a splash.

Fry until the tofu is golden and crispy then remove with a sieve and place on paper towel to soak up any excess oil. Finish with the spring onion and serve with your favourite dipping sauce.

TIP: To check the oil temperature, simply stick a wooden chopstick in the oil, and when it is immediately surrounded by tiny bubbles, the oil is hot enough. Of course, you can also add just one tofu cube to test the temperature. When it floats and is fried within 5 seconds the oil is ready for frying.

PREPARATION TIME
5 minutes

SERVES
1

This marinated silken tofu recipe is definitely one of the easiest and quickest tofu recipes there is. It requires only a handful of ingredients and 5 minutes of your time. Despite being so simple, the super smooth and savoury taste of this dish will surprise you.

鹽澆丝绸豆腐

MARINATED SILKEN TOFU

300 g (10½ oz) silken tofu

3 tablespoons soy sauce

1 garlic clove, finely chopped

5 g (⅛ oz) piece of fresh ginger, peeled and finely chopped

1 spring onion (scallion), finely sliced

2 tablespoons canola (rapeseed) oil

1 tablespoon sesame oil

To remove the tofu from the packet, open the top, turn a plate upside down and place it over the tofu. Carefully flip the packet and plate so the tofu can be transferred to the plate. If it doesn't come out, cut a small opening on all four corners of the packet then lift the packet gently off the tofu. Add the soy sauce, garlic, ginger and spring onion to the top of the tofu.

Heat the oils in a saucepan over a high heat. Once it is very hot – about 180°C (360°F) on a cooking thermometer – pour it over the tofu.

PREPARATION TIME
15 minutes

COOKING TIME
20 minutes

SERVES
2

Pan-fried tofu with fresh chilli is one of the most common home dishes from Hunan. As in many other Hunanese dishes, fresh green chilli is used rather than dried chilli. The tofu is first pan-fried then stir-fried with garlic and chilli, making it slightly spicy, crispy and juicy. And as I described in my story (see page 8), this was probably the first dish I ever prepared myself.

青椒煎豆腐

PAN-FRIED TOFU WITH FRESH GREEN CHILLI

90 ml (3 fl oz) canola (rapeseed) oil

500 g (1 lb 2 oz) tender tofu, cut into 1 cm (½ in) thick slices

4 garlic cloves, finely chopped

200 g (7 oz) fresh green chilli, destemmed and chopped

3 tablespoons soy sauce

1 spring onion (scallion), finely sliced

Heat a wok over a medium–high heat. Once hot, add 60 ml (2 fl oz/¼ cup) of the oil and tilt the wok to distribute evenly. Add the tofu and pan-fry on both sides until golden, then take it out.

Add the remaining oil to the wok with the garlic and stir for 30 seconds, then add the chilli and stir for about 1 minute.

Add the pan-fried tofu and soy sauce, mixing everything together well, then cook for 2–3 minutes. Add the spring onion and serve.

PREPARATION TIME
15 minutes

COOKING TIME
20 minutes

SERVES
2

Sweet and sour dishes are popular in many southern regions of China. Compared to many other savoury and spicy tofu dishes, the tofu in this recipe is first pan-fried until it is crispy, then cooked in the sweet–sour sauce until tender. After cooking, the tofu becomes very succulent and moreish.

糖醋豆腐

SWEET AND SOUR TOFU

500 g (1 lb 2 oz) tender or firm tofu, cut into 2 cm (¾ in) dice

80 g (2¾ oz) cornflour (cornstarch), plus 1 teaspoon extra

1 tablespoon sugar

¼ teaspoon salt

2 tablespoons soy sauce

3 tablespoons Chinese dark vinegar or rice vinegar

80 g (2¾ oz) tomato sauce (ketchup)

120 ml (4 fl oz) canola (rapeseed) oil

2 garlic cloves, finely chopped

1 spring onion (scallion), finely sliced

Coat the tofu in 80 g (2¾ oz) cornflour. In a bowl, mix together the sugar, salt, soy sauce, Chinese dark vinegar, tomato sauce, remaining cornflour and 100 ml (3½ fl oz) water.

Heat a wok over a medium–high heat. Once hot, add 90 ml (3 fl oz) of the oil. Add the tofu and pan-fry on both sides until golden and crispy, then take it out. Note, the tofu dice might stick together because of the starch. Just separate them carefully with a spatula or chopsticks when pan-frying.

Add the remaining oil and the garlic and stir for 30 seconds, then return the tofu to the wok and add the soy sauce mixture. Let it cook for a few minutes until the sauce has reduced by two-thirds and the remaining sauce has thickened, then add the spring onion.

Tofu and spring onion (scallion) are a match made in heaven. Spring onion is almost always needed in tofu dishes, as it brings out extra flavour in the tofu. Spring onion tofu is a popular home dish that requires very few ingredients: the tofu is simply simmered in a sauce with lots of spring onion until tender, juicy and full of flavour. It is also one of the quickest tofu dishes to cook if you don't have much time to prepare a meal.

葱燜豆腐

SPRING ONION TOFU

3 tablespoons soy sauce

2 tablespoons vegan oyster sauce

½ teaspoon cornflour (cornstarch) or potato starch

60 ml (2 fl oz/¼ cup) canola (rapeseed) oil

2 garlic cloves, finely chopped

10 g (¼ oz) piece of fresh ginger, peeled and finely chopped

500 g (1 lb 2 oz) tender tofu, cut into 1.5 cm (½ in) dice

3 spring onions (scallions), roughly sliced

In a bowl, mix together the soy sauce, vegan oyster sauce and starch until well combined.

Heat a wok over a medium heat and, once hot, add the oil. Add the garlic and ginger and stir for 30 seconds, then add the tofu dice, moving them gently so they don't break or stick to the pan. After 1 minute add the soy sauce mixture and stir gently.

Cover with a lid and allow to cook for 3–5 minutes, gently tilting the pan occasionally to avoid the tofu sticking. Remove the lid and add the spring onion. Let it cook until most of the sauce is gone.

Five spice (see page 27) is one of the most classic Chinese spice blends. It normally consists of cinnamon, star anise, sichuan peppercorns, fennel seeds and cloves. Store-bought versions sometimes include other spices too. This five-spice tofu is super delicious and juicy, and it makes a great snack or appetiser to share with friends and family.

五香豆干
FIVE-SPICE TOFU

120 ml (4 fl oz) canola (rapeseed) oil

1 kg (2 lb 3 oz) tender or firm tofu, cut into 1 cm (½ in) thick slices

30 g (1 oz) piece of fresh ginger, peeled and sliced

½ onion, sliced

2 cinnamon sticks

6 star anise

1 tablespoon sichuan peppercorns

1 tablespoon fennel seeds

1 tablespoon cloves

5 dried bay leaves

10 chilli flakes

50 g (1¾ oz) crystal sugar, crushed

120 ml (4 fl oz) soy sauce

60 ml (2 fl oz/¼ cup) vegan oyster sauce

480 ml (16 fl oz) hot water

1 tablespoon dark soy sauce

Heat a wok over a medium heat and, once hot, add the oil and pan-fry the tofu until both sides are golden and crispy. Remove and set aside.

Add the ginger and onion, stir for 30 seconds, then add all the spices and dried chilli and stir for 1 minute until the aromas of the spices come out. Add the crystal sugar and stir for another minute.

Return the tofu to the wok and add the soy sauce, vegan oyster sauce and hot water, then add the dark soy sauce. Cover with a lid and let it cook for a few minutes, stirring occasionally.

When the sauce has reduced by two-thirds, turn off the heat. This dish can be served hot or cold, eaten as a side dish to rice or as a snack.

This tofu skin salad is one of my favourite dishes in summer. The different textures and flavours of all the ingredients come together in one bowl and match perfectly with one another. It is very refreshing, slightly spicy and full of flavour.

PREPARATION TIME
10 minutes

COOKING TIME
5 minutes

SERVES
2

涼拌豆皮

TOFU SKIN SALAD

Boil the tofu skin in a saucepan for 1 minute, then take it out.

Add the carrot and boil for 30 seconds, then remove and add the bean sprouts. Boil for 15 seconds, then drain.

Heat a wok over a medium heat. Once hot, add the oil and garlic. Stir for 15 seconds, then turn off the heat. Add the soy sauce, Chinese dark vinegar and chilli oil.

Add the tofu skin, carrot, bean sprouts, fresh chilli, cucumber, sesame and spring onion, if using, and mix everything together well before serving.

250 g (9 oz) fresh tofu skin, finely sliced

1 carrot, peeled and finely sliced

100 g (3½ oz) bean sprouts

2 tablespoons canola (rapeseed) oil

3 garlic cloves, finely chopped

60 ml (2 fl oz/¼ cup) soy sauce

60 ml (2 fl oz/¼ cup) Chinese dark vinegar

2 tablespoons Chilli oil (page 29)

60 g (2 oz) fresh chilli, destemmed and finely sliced

200 g (7 oz) cucumber, finely sliced

1 tablespoon toasted sesame seeds (optional)

1 spring onion (scallion), cut into pieces (optional)

PREPARATION TIME
10 minutes

COOKING TIME
5 minutes

SERVES
2

The elastic and chewy hard-pressed tofu sheets are first boiled then cooked quickly in a sauce here, absorbing all the different flavours. It is super easy and very tasty.

辣酱豆皮

SPICY TOFU SKIN

250 g (9 oz) fresh tofu skin or pressed tofu sheets, cut into 1 cm (½ in) wide noodles

2 tablespoons canola (rapeseed) oil

4 garlic cloves, finely chopped

5 g (⅛ oz) piece of fresh ginger, peeled and finely chopped

1 tablespoon Laoganma Chilli Sauce with Fermented Soybean

1 tablespoon Chilli oil (page 29)

3 tablespoons soy sauce

3 tablespoons Chinese dark vinegar

1 spring onion (scallion), cut into short lengths

Boil the tofu skin for 1 minute, then remove the tofu skin and set aside.

Heat a wok over a medium–high heat and, once hot, add the oil, garlic and ginger and stir-fry for about 30 seconds. Add the Laoganma and chilli oil, stir for 15 seconds, then add the soy sauce and dark vinegar and stir everything together.

When the sauce starts simmering, add the tofu skin and stir quickly so it's evenly covered with sauce, then add the spring onion.

Tofu puffs are essentially deep-fried tofu. The best kind of tofu for tofu puffs is firm tofu made with nigari salt as the coagulant. The porous texture makes them a perfect ingredient for any dish with a sauce, as the fluffy puffs will absorb a lot of the sauce during cooking and become succulent and flavourful.

青椒蒜苋油豆腐

FRIED TOFU PUFFS WITH GREEN CHILLI AND GARLIC SCAPES

3 tablespoons canola (rapeseed) oil

3 garlic cloves, sliced

200 g (7 oz) garlic scapes, cut into 3 cm (1¼ in) lengths

250 g (9 oz) fried tofu puffs, halved

2 tablespoons soy sauce

1 tablespoon vegan oyster sauce

1 teaspoon cornflour (cornstarch) or potato starch

60 ml (2 fl oz/¼ cup) warm water

100 g (3½ oz) fresh green chilli, destemmed and sliced

1 spring onion (scallion), cut into short lengths

Heat a wok over a medium–high heat and, once hot, add the oil, garlic and garlic scapes. Stir-fry for 1 minute, then add the tofu puffs and stir for a little before adding the soy sauce and vegan oyster sauce. Stir-fry for another 30 seconds. Mix the starch with the warm water and add it to the wok. Mix everything well.

Stir-fry for 2–3 minutes until most of the sauce is absorbed by the tofu puffs. Add the chilli and stir for another minute before adding the spring onion.

PREPARATION TIME
15 minutes

COOKING TIME
10 minutes

SERVES
2

Guota tofu is a traditional dish originally from Shandong province. Guota (鍋塌) is a cooking method in Shandong cuisine that sees the main ingredient dipped in egg before being pan-fried then cooked in a seasoned broth or sauce. Here, I have used cornflour (cornstarch) and sparkling water instead of the eggs. The tofu is very crispy after the pan-frying, and becomes super juicy and savoury after being cooked again in the sauce.

鍋塌豆腐

GUOTA TOFU

500 g (1 lb 2 oz) tender or semi-firm tofu, cut into 1 cm (½ in) thick slices

250 ml (8½ fl oz/1 cup) sparkling soda water (club soda)

100 g (3½ oz) cornflour (cornstarch)

120 ml (4 fl oz) canola (rapeseed) oil

3 garlic cloves, sliced

15 g (½ oz) piece of fresh ginger, peeled and sliced in long, thin strips

250 ml (8½ fl oz/1 cup) warm water

3 tablespoons soy sauce

2 tablespoons vegan oyster sauce

2 fresh red chillies, destemmed and sliced

1 spring onion (scallion), sliced

Dip the tofu first in the sparkling water then coat evenly in the cornflour. Heat a wok and, once hot, add 90 ml (3 fl oz) of the oil and pan-fry the tofu until both sides are golden. Remove and set aside.

Add the remaining oil and fry the garlic and ginger over a medium heat for 30 seconds. Add the fried tofu, mix, then add the water, soy sauce and vegan oyster sauce. Mix the tofu well with the sauce.

Allow the sauce to come to the boil, then reduce the heat to low and simmer for a few minutes, stirring carefully so the tofu doesn't stick to the wok.

When most of the sauce has been absorbed by the tofu, add the chilli, mix, and let it simmer for 1 more minute, then add the spring onion.

ALL ABOUT VEGGIES

In this chapter I will share some of the popular vegetable dishes in China, including some of the most common veggies, like eggplant (aubergine) and potato, and some of the more special vegetables, such as lotus root, bamboo shoots, taro and winter melon (wax melon).

Most of the recipes in this chapter are southern dishes, as the variety of vegetables is much larger in the south, especially in regions where the winter is relatively warm and short, for example in Guangdong and Fujian. In the north, the most popular vegetables are more basic: Chinese cabbage (wombok), daikon (white radish), potatoes and carrots. These used to be the only vegetables available during the long northern winter, and most families had a cellar to store them in during the harshest weather.

Nowadays, people in the north have access to many other vegetables during winter, but old methods of vegetable preservation have become an important part of the local food culture. In northeast China, almost every family would pickle a large amount of Chinese cabbage to prepare for winter. Large urns are filled with Chinese cabbage, water and salt. Instead of a lid, a large stone is put on top to prevent the cabbage from floating and it is left to ferment for 2–4 weeks depending on the temperature. Pickled Chinese cabbage has long been an essential ingredient in northeastern Chinese cooking, used in stews, soups, dumplings, noodles and stir-fries.

In Beijing, preserved vegetables (酱菜) have also become a local specialty. There are dozens of different vegetables that are regularly pickled, some of the most popular being cucumber, daikon, Chinese artichoke, brown mustard and turnip. Unlike the pickled vegetables from most regions in China which are normally pickled with salt and water – sometimes with chilli and other spices – Beijing pickled vegetables are often pickled with sauces, such as soybean sauce, sweet bean sauce and soy sauce. Sometimes they are even cooked in a sauce, therefore many of the preserved vegetables are a dark colour. The Beijing preserved vegetables are not very salty or very sweet, which makes them the perfect side dish with rice, noodles, congee and many other dishes.

There are many ways to prepare different kinds of vegetables. Root vegetables are generally rich in starch and, therefore, take longer to cook, making them suitable for stews, soups and braised dishes, but some root vegetables, like lotus root, yam and arrowhead tuber, are often thinly sliced and stir-fried.

Eggplant is definitely one of the most popular vegetables in Chinese cuisine. Its spongy texture makes it cook slowly, absorbing the oil, therefore it requires more oil to cook than most other vegetables. For most eggplant dishes, the eggplant is deep-fried, pan-fried or steamed before being cooked again with other ingredients and sauces. Deep-fried eggplant usually tastes better when it is cooked twice, but if you don't want to deep-fry at home, you can just pan-fry the eggplant with more oil than a normal stir-fried dish. The best eggplants to use in Chinese cooking are the long ones, which are light purple in colour. These eggplants have a thin peel and tender texture, making them easy to cook. They become especially juicy and succulent when cooked in sauces.

Bamboo shoots are another special vegetable that's important in Chinese cuisine. Their season ranges from winter to early spring. The winter bamboo shoots are found buried in the earth, dug out, and are normally thicker and more solid than spring bamboo shoots. They have a richer umami taste and are used mostly in stews, soups, hot pot and stir-fries. Spring bamboo shoots, given a few months of growth, are much longer and thinner in size, and are grown above the ground so they can be easily spotted. The spring bamboo shoots are hollow in the middle and have a more refreshing taste and crunchier texture than winter bamboo shoots. They work perfectly in stir-fries or braises. If you purchase fresh bamboo shoots, it is very important to cook them as soon as possible, as they become more fibrous and the taste is not as good if you wait too long before using them.

Leafy greens, such as water spinach, spinach, pak choi, you mai cai, kai lan and choy sum, are the quickest and easiest vegetables to cook. In order to preserve the nutrients at their best, these leafy greens are quickly stir-fried over a high heat, normally with chopped garlic and salt, and sometimes also with a sauce. Seasonal leafy greens stir-fried with garlic are among the most basic of dishes that can be found in any Chinese restaurant.

Although not counted as vegetables, mushrooms are also very popular in Chinese cuisine, especially in the Yunnan region, where there is a huge variety of edible wild mushrooms. In other parts of China, king oyster mushrooms and oyster mushrooms are some of the most common mushrooms used in cooking. They are succulent, tasty and easy to cook, making them ideal for stir-fries, stews, soups and hot pot.

Yuxiang eggplant (aubergine) is definitely the most well known and popular eggplant dish in China. Yuxiang is a famous seasoning mixture in Sichuan cuisine – typically savoury, sweet, sour and slightly spicy. It literally means 'fish fragrance', allegedly because the eggplant was originally cooked in chilli pickled with fish. Despite its name, the recipe nowadays has nothing to do with fish.

Traditionally the eggplant is first deep-fried then cooked in the yuxiang sauce. If you don't like deep-frying, you can also mix the eggplant strips with half a teaspoon of salt and let it marinate for 15 minutes until the liquid comes out. Squeeze all the water out and pan-fry the eggplant until it's golden and cooked on the outside.

魚香茄子

YUXIANG EGGPLANT

560 ml (19 fl oz/2¼ cups) canola (rapeseed) oil

750 g (1 lb 11 oz) eggplant (aubergine), sliced 4 cm (1½ in) long and 1 cm (½ in) wide

2 tablespoons soy sauce

3 tablespoons Chinese dark vinegar

1 tablespoon sugar

1 tablespoon Chinese cooking wine

½ teaspoon potato starch or cornflour (cornstarch)

3 garlic cloves, finely chopped

20 g (¾ oz) piece of fresh ginger, peeled and finely chopped

50 g (1¾ oz) pickled Sichuan chilli or piri piri, finely chopped

1 spring onion (scallion), sliced

Heat 480 ml (16 fl oz) of the oil in a saucepan over a medium–high heat. To check the oil is hot enough for deep-frying, hold a wooden chopstick in the oil. If it is immediately surrounded by tiny bubbles, the oil is ready to use.

Deep-fry the eggplant until it is soft and a bit golden on the outside, then remove. Deep-fry the eggplant for the second time, but only for 30 seconds (this can be done immediately after removing the eggplant from the first deep-fry). Deep-frying it twice helps to reduce the oil absorbed by the eggplant.

In a bowl, mix the soy sauce, Chinese dark vinegar, sugar, cooking wine and starch.

Heat the wok over a medium heat and, once hot, add the remaining oil. Add the garlic and ginger, stir for 30 seconds, then add the pickled chilli and stir-fry for 1 minute. Then add the eggplant and continue stirring for another minute.

Add the sauce to the wok and keep stirring until most of the sauce has been absorbed by the eggplant. Add the spring onion.

PREPARATION TIME
15 minutes

COOKING TIME
15 minutes

SERVES
2

To make this dish, eggplant (aubergine) is first coated in a bit of starch then pan-fried, then quickly cooked in a sweet-sour sauce. The eggplant is succulent and full of flavour, and it goes very well with rice.

糖醋茄子

SWEET AND SOUR EGGPLANT

550 g (1 lb 3 oz) eggplant (aubergine), sliced 4 cm (1½ in) long and 1 cm (½ in) wide

3 tablespoons potato starch or cornflour (cornstarch), plus 1 teaspoon extra

3 tablespoons soy sauce

1½ tablespoons vegan oyster sauce

3 tablespoons Chinese dark vinegar

1 tablespoon sugar

150 ml (5 fl oz) canola (rapeseed) oil

3 garlic cloves, finely chopped

20 g (¾ oz) piece of fresh ginger, peeled and finely chopped

1 spring onion (scallion), sliced

Coat the eggplant evenly with 3 tablespoons of the starch. In a bowl, mix together the soy sauce, vegan oyster sauce, dark vinegar, sugar and remaining starch.

Heat a wok over a medium–high heat and, once hot, add 120 ml (4 fl oz) of the oil. Add the eggplant and pan-fry for a few minutes until it's slightly brown and cooked, then remove.

Add the remaining oil along with the garlic and ginger and stir for 30 seconds. Return the eggplant to the wok and add the sauce. Let it cook for 2–3 minutes until most of the sauce is gone, then garnish with the spring onion.

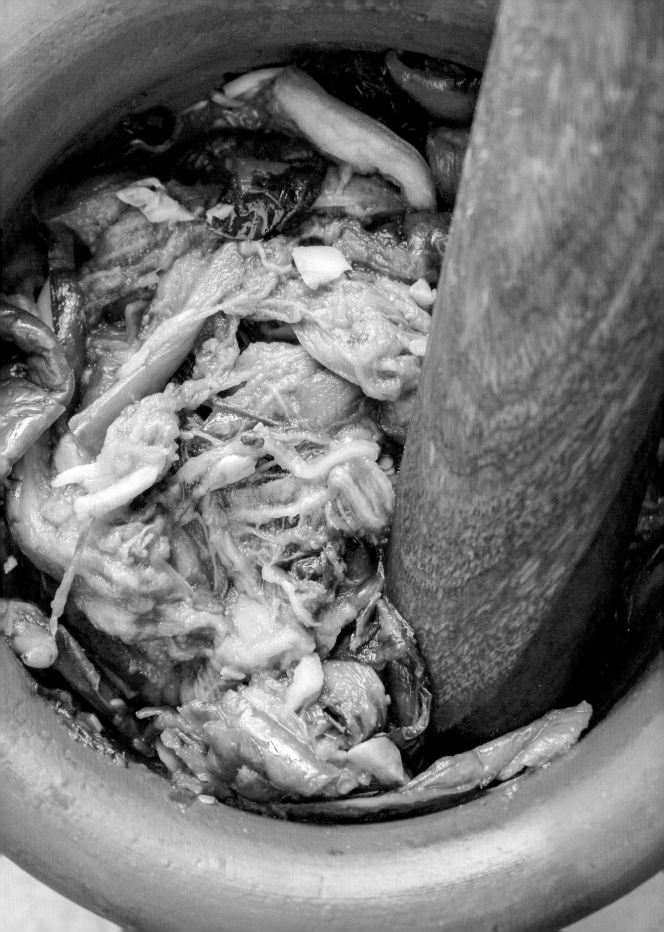

Pestled eggplant (aubergine) with green chilli is a popular home dish from Hunan. Originally the fresh chilli would be grilled over charcoal until the peel was burnt, then peeled and smashed together with steamed eggplant and other seasonings using a mortar and pestle. It is a very quick and easy dish, great as an appetiser for dinner.

擂辣椒茄子

PESTLED EGGPLANT WITH GREEN CHILLI

300 g (10½ oz) eggplant (aubergine), sliced

3 tablespoons canola (rapeseed) oil

200 g (7 oz) fresh green chilli, destemmed

3 garlic cloves, finely chopped

60 ml (2 fl oz/¼ cup) soy sauce

3 tablespoons Chinese dark vinegar

½ teaspoon salt

Fill a saucepan with hot water and place a steam rack in the pot (the water level should not be higher than the steam rack). Place the eggplant on a plate on the steam rack, cover with a lid and let it steam over a high heat for 15 minutes.

Heat a wok over a medium heat and, once hot, add the oil. Add the chilli and pan-fry until the outside of the chilli is charred and brown. Add the garlic and stir for 15 seconds, then turn off the heat.

Combine all the ingredients in a mortar, smash everything together with a pestle then serve.

Stir-fried eggplant (aubergine) with green beans is a popular home dish from Hunan. As the name suggests, it consists of two main ingredients, which are stir-fried together with a bit of sauce. Yard-long (metre) beans are normally used for this dish. They are long green beans that can grow more than 1 metre (3.3 feet) in length, hence the name. Yard-long beans are a popular vegetable in summer and they are also used very commonly in pickling. Since yard-long beans are a very seasonal vegetable and might be hard to come by for many, I have replaced them with green beans for this recipe.

豆角茄子

STIR-FRIED EGGPLANT WITH GREEN BEANS

300 g (10½ oz) eggplant (aubergine), sliced 4 cm (1½ in) long and 1 cm (½ in) wide

90 ml (3 fl oz) canola (rapeseed) oil

200 g (7 oz) green beans or yard-long (metre) beans, cut into 3 cm (1¼ in) lengths

3 garlic cloves, finely chopped

2 tablespoons soy sauce

3 tablespoons vegan oyster sauce

1 spring onion (scallion), sliced

Fill a saucepan with hot water and place a steam rack in the pot (the water level should not be higher than the steam rack). Place the eggplant on a plate on the steam rack, cover with a lid and let it steam over a high heat for 5 minutes.

Heat a wok over a medium–high heat and, once hot, add 60 ml (2 fl oz/¼ cup) of the oil. Add the steamed eggplant, stir for a few minutes until it's slightly brown and cooked, then remove. Add the remaining oil and the beans and stir for a few minutes until they're slightly brown and cooked.

Add the garlic and stir for 1 minute. Add the soy sauce and vegan oyster sauce and stir for 1–2 minutes until the sauce has been mostly absorbed by the eggplant, then add the spring onion.

Lantern eggplant (aubergine) is a popular dish during Chinese New Year, since traditionally red lanterns are hung during the festival and the shape of the eggplant resembles a lantern. The best kind of eggplant to use for this dish is the long purple eggplant which is about 5 cm (2 in) thick. Avoid using eggplants that are too thin or thick, otherwise the cooking might be tricky.

PREPARATION TIME
15 minutes

COOKING TIME
15 minutes

SERVES
2

炸饢豆腐茄子

LANTERN EGGPLANT FILLED WITH TOFU

Smash the tofu and mix it with 2 tablespoons of the soy sauce, the vegan oyster sauce, cooking wine and starch.

Cut the eggplant into large pieces about 3 cm (1¼ in) long, then score each piece five times, with the cuts about 5 mm (¼ in) apart. Fill the slits with the seasoned tofu.

Heat the oil in a large saucepan. To check the oil is hot enough for deep-frying, hold a wooden chopstick in the oil. If it is immediately surrounded by tiny bubbles, the oil is ready to use. Deep-fry the tofu-filled eggplant for a few minutes until it is golden on the outside, then remove and place on a serving dish.

Heat a saucepan over a medium heat. Add 1 tablespoon oil and the garlic and stir for 15 seconds, then add the rice vinegar, tomato sauce, sugar, remaining soy sauce and 2 tablespoons water. Bring to the boil over a medium heat, then pour the sauce over the lantern eggplant and scatter over the spring onion.

150 g (5½ oz) tender or firm tofu

60 ml (2 fl oz/¼ cup) soy sauce

1 tablespoon vegan oyster sauce

2 tablespoons Chinese cooking wine

2 teaspoons potato starch or cornflour (or cornstarch)

400 g (14 oz) long purple eggplant (aubergine)

360 ml (12 fl oz) canola (rapeseed) oil, plus 1 tablespoon extra

3 garlic cloves, finely chopped

1 teaspoon rice vinegar

2 tablespoons tomato sauce (ketchup)

1 teaspoon sugar

1 spring onion (scallion), sliced

Eggplant (aubergine) is one of the most popular vegetables at late-night barbecue stands in China. In this recipe, we grill the eggplant in the oven with the same seasonings as those used in barbecue dishes. It can be served as an appetiser for dinner or can be eaten as a snack.

蒜蓉烤茄子

GRILLED EGGPLANT WITH GARLIC

400g (14 oz) long purple eggplant (aubergine)

60 ml (2 fl oz/¼ cup) canola (rapeseed) oil, plus extra for brushing

5 garlic cloves, finely chopped

2 bird's eye chillies, destemmed and finely chopped

2 tablespoons chilli flakes

1 tablespoon cumin seeds

60 ml (2 fl oz/¼ cup) soy sauce

1 tablespoon vegan oyster sauce

1 spring onion (scallion), roughly chopped

Preheat the oven to 200°C (390°F).

Brush a thin layer of the oil on the outside of the eggplant, then place them on a baking tray on the middle rack of the oven. Bake for 15 minutes, then turn them around and cook for another 10 minutes.

In a bowl, mix the garlic, chilli, chilli flakes, cumin, soy sauce, vegan oyster sauce and the oil. Put the eggplants on a baking tray, cut them open lengthways and flatten, then brush the seasoning evenly over the eggplants. Bake for another 6–8 minutes then remove and scatter over the spring onion.

PREPARATION TIME
20 minutes

COOKING TIME
20 minutes

SERVES
2

This is another dish cooked using a clay pot. The juicy eggplant (aubergine), elastic glass noodles and slightly spicy and savoury sauce make a great combination, and the clay pot brings all the flavours together well at the last stage of cooking.

茄子粉丝煲

CLAY POT EGGPLANT WITH GLASS NOODLES

100 g (3½ oz) glass or mung bean noodles

½ teaspoon salt

500 g (1 lb 2 oz) eggplant (aubergine), sliced 3 cm (1¼ in) long and 1 cm (½ in) wide

120 ml (4 fl oz) canola (rapeseed) oil

4 garlic cloves, finely chopped

15 g (½ oz) piece of fresh ginger, peeled and finely chopped

1 onion, finely sliced

5 pickled chillies (see page 31), chopped

3 tablespoons soy sauce

2 tablespoons vegan oyster sauce

1 tablespoon Chinese dark vinegar

90 ml (3 fl oz) warm water

1 spring onion (scallion), sliced

Soak the glass noodles in water for 15 minutes, then drain. Sprinkle the salt on the eggplant, massaging it in evenly. Set aside for 10 minutes, then squeeze the liquid out of the eggplant.

Heat a wok over a medium–high heat and, once hot, add 90 ml (3 fl oz) of the oil. Add the eggplant and stir-fry for a few minutes until it is cooked and slightly brown on the outside. Take it out.

Add the remaining oil and the garlic, then 15 seconds later add the ginger, onion and pickled chillies. Add the glass noodles followed by the soy sauce, vegan oyster sauce and dark vinegar, then mix everything together well and add the warm water.

Put everything into a cold clay pot, cover with the lid and let it cook for a few minutes over a low heat until most of the sauce has been reduced. Finish with the spring onion.

Dry-fried green beans is definitely the most beloved green bean recipe in Chinese cuisine, originally from Sichuan. Dry-frying is a cooking method in which the ingredients are fried in oil until cooked without adding any water, Chinese cooking wine or soup. The beans here are first dry-fried then cooked quickly a second time with other ingredients. The beans are savoury and slightly crunchy, and the dried chilli is crispy. It's a great dish to serve with rice.

乾煸四季豆

DRY-FRIED GREEN BEANS

Heat a wok over a high heat and, once hot, add 60 ml (2 fl oz/¼ cup) of the oil and the beans. Stir for a few minutes until the beans are brown and wrinkly on the outside, then take them out.

Add the remaining oil with the sichuan peppercorns and stir for 15 seconds, then add the garlic and stir for 30 seconds before adding the dried chilli. Stir for another 30 seconds.

Add the green beans and stir for 1–2 minutes until the beans are all cooked, then add the soy sauce and stir for another 1–2 minutes.

90 ml (3 fl oz) canola (rapeseed) oil

500 g (1 lb 2 oz) green beans, cut into 4 cm (1½ in) lengths

1 teaspoon sichuan peppercorns

4 garlic cloves, roughly chopped

5 dried chillies, destemmed and cut into short lengths

3 tablespoons soy sauce

Dì san xian is the most popular vegetable dish from the northeast of China. The name roughly translates to 'three delicacies from the earth' because it consists of three key ingredients: eggplant (aubergine), potato and sweet peppers.

地三鲜
DI SAN XIAN

500 g (1 lb 2 oz) waxy potatoes, peeled and cut into medium chunks

300 g (10½ oz) eggplant (aubergine), cut into chunks

3 tablespoons soy sauce

3 tablespoons vegan oyster sauce

½ teaspoon sugar

½ teaspoon cornflour (cornstarch)

150 ml (5 fl oz) canola (rapeseed) oil, plus extra if needed

200 g (7 oz) green capsicum (bell pepper), cut into short lengths

3 garlic cloves, roughly chopped

½ onion, cut into short lengths

1 spring onion (scallion), sliced

Fill a saucepan with hot water and place a steam rack in the pot (the water level should not be higher than the steam rack). Place the potato on a plate on the steam rack, cover with a lid and let it steam over a high heat for 12 minutes, then remove. Add the eggplant, cover with a lid and steam for 3 minutes.

In a bowl, mix together the soy sauce, vegan oyster sauce, sugar and cornflour with 1 tablespoon water.

Heat a wok over a medium–high heat and, once hot, add the oil and pan-fry the potatoes until golden and crispy on the outside, then remove. Pan-fry the eggplant until it's cooked and a bit brown on the outside, then take the eggplant out. Add the pepper and fry for about 1 minute until it is a bit cooked and wrinkly on the outside. Remove and set aside.

Add a bit more oil to the wok if necessary, then add the garlic and stir-fry for 15 seconds before adding the onion and frying for 30 seconds. Add the potato, eggplant and pepper and stir-fry for another minute.

Add the sauce and cook for another 3–5 minutes until most of the sauce has evaporated. Add the spring onion and serve.

Grandma potato is a famous dish from Yunnan. The dish got its name because the potatoes are so soft and smooth that even toothless grandmas wouldn't have a problem eating it. It is a sour, spicy and very appetising dish.

老奶洋芋

GRANDMA POTATO

1 kg (2 lb 3 oz) potatoes, peeled and cut into 1 cm (½ in) dice

6 garlic cloves, finely chopped

60 ml (2 fl oz/¼ cup) warm water

120 ml (4 fl oz) canola (rapeseed) oil

8 pickled chillies (see page 31), roughly chopped

100 g (3½ oz) preserved or pickled mustard, finely chopped

2 tablespoons rice vinegar

2 tablespoons soy sauce

1 teaspoon salt

½ teaspoon ground white pepper

1 spring onion (scallion), sliced

Fill a saucepan with hot water and place a steam rack in the pot (the water level should not be higher than the steam rack). Place the potato on a plate on the steam rack, cover with a lid and let it steam over a high heat for 20 minutes. Remove, then smash two-thirds of the potato dice.

Add half of the garlic to a small bowl with the warm water.

Heat a wok over a medium–high heat and, once hot, add the oil and the remaining garlic. Stir for 30 seconds then add the pickled chilli and, 15 seconds later, add the preserved mustard and stir-fry for 1 minute.

Add the smashed potato and stir-fry for 1 minute then add the potato dice. Stir for another minute then add the soaked garlic and its soaking water, plus the vinegar, and stir-fry for 1–2 minutes.

Add the soy sauce and stir-fry for 1 minute then add the salt and ground white pepper, stir for 1–2 minutes, then add the spring onion.

This is one of the most popular potato dishes in China, cooked by almost every family. It's quick and easy, but it does require some cutting skills to cut the potato strips evenly. The potato is slightly crunchy, sour and spicy. The key to maintaining the crunchiness is to cook the potato quickly over the highest heat. If the heat is not strong enough, the potato will turn soggy before it's cooked.

酸辣土豆丝

SOUR AND SPICY POTATO STRIPS

1 × 300 g (10½ oz) waxy potato, peeled and cut into thin strips

60 ml (2 fl oz/¼ cup) canola (rapeseed) oil

1 teaspoon sichuan peppercorns

3 garlic cloves, thinly sliced

8 pickled chillies (see page 31), roughly chopped

3 tablespoons rice vinegar

½ teaspoon salt

1 spring onion (scallion), sliced

Soak the potato strips in cold water or rinse them under running water. This step is to remove the extra starch. Drain well.

Heat a wok over a high heat and, once hot, add the oil. Add the sichuan peppercorns and stir for 10 seconds, then add the garlic and pickled chilli and stir for 30 seconds.

Add the potato and stir-fry for about 2 minutes until it changes colour and becomes translucent. Add the rice vinegar and keep stir-frying for another 1–2 minutes before adding the salt. Give it a quick stir then add the spring onion.

This spring onion (scallion) potato pancake is very aromatic, crispy and yummy. It has a similar taste and texture to hash browns. The potato is first thinly grated then mixed with spices and pan-fried until golden and crispy. Salt is sprinkled on the pancake after it's done – if the salt is added before, it will make the pancake soggy.

PREPARATION TIME
10 minutes

COOKING TIME
10 minutes

SERVES
2

土豆怂餅

SPRING ONION POTATO PANCAKE

In a big bowl, combine the potato, sichuan peppercorns, five spice, spring onion and cornflour. Mix everything together well.

Heat a non-stick frying pan over a medium–high heat and, once hot, add the oil. Let it heat up a bit then add the seasoned potato. Use a spatula to form it into a flat pancake.

Fry for about 3–5 minutes until the bottom of the pancake is golden and crispy, then carefully flip the pancake over and pan-fry the other side until it's also golden and crispy. Remove the pancake from the pan and sprinkle with the salt.

500 g (1 lb 2 oz) potatoes, peeled and thinly grated

½ teaspoon ground sichuan peppercorns

1 teaspoon five spice (see page 27)

1 spring onion (scallion), cut into short lengths

1 teaspoon cornflour (cornstarch)

3 tablespoons canola (rapeseed) oil

½ teaspoon salt

PREPARATION TIME
10 minutes

COOKING TIME
10 minutes

SERVES
2

These wave-shaped potato strips are a very popular street food in Yunnan and Sichuan. They have a very unique name - Lang Ya (狼牙), which means 'wolf teeth' in Chinese. The potato is first cut into thick slices, then cut with a wave-shaped knife to obtain the shape. You can also just use crinkle-cut fries as a shortcut.

狼牙土豆

WOLF TOOTH POTATO

400 g (14 oz) waxy potatoes or crinkle-cut fries

480 ml (16 fl oz) canola (rapeseed) oil, for deep-frying

3 garlic cloves, finely chopped

¼ teaspoon salt

2 tablespoons soy sauce

1 tablespoon Chinese dark vinegar

2 tablespoons Chilli oil (page 29)

1 teaspoon five spice (see page 27)

1 tablespoon cumin seeds or ground cumin

1 spring onion (scallion), sliced

1 coriander (cilantro) sprig, cut into short lengths

Peel the potato, then cut it first into 1 cm (½ in) thick slices, then into wave-shaped strips about the size of French fries. If you use crinkle-cut fries then skip this step.

Heat the oil in a large saucepan. To check the oil is hot enough for deep-frying, hold a wooden chopstick in the oil. If it is immediately surrounded by tiny bubbles, the oil is ready to use. Deep-fry the potato strips until golden and crispy, then remove and place on a piece of paper towel to drain.

Put the potato strips in a big bowl and add the remaining ingredients. Mix everything together well.

PREPARATION TIME
15 minutes

COOKING TIME
20 minutes

SERVES
2

These potato slices are first pan-fried until they are slightly brown and crispy, then stir-fried again with garlic, chilli oil and cumin seeds. The cumin adds a very unique aroma to the dish and makes it extra flavourful.

孜然土豆片

SLICED POTATO WITH CUMIN

500 g (1 lb 2 oz) waxy potatoes, peeled and cut into 5 mm (¼ in) slices

90 ml (3 fl oz) canola (rapeseed) oil

4 garlic cloves, sliced

1 tablespoon Chilli oil (page 29)

2 tablespoons cumin seeds

2 tablespoons soy sauce

1 tablespoon vegan oyster sauce

1 spring onion (scallion), sliced

Rinse the potato slices quickly to get rid of any extra starch.

Heat a wok over a medium–high heat and, once hot, add the oil. Add the potato slices and pan-fry for a few minutes until golden and crispy, then remove.

Add the garlic and stir for 30 seconds. Add the chilli oil and cumin seeds and stir for 1 minute until fragrant, then return the potato slices to the wok with the soy sauce and vegan oyster sauce. Mix everything together well, stirring for 1–2 minutes, then add the spring onion.

The unique water plant lotus (*Nelumbo nucifera*) has had great significance in Chinese culture for more than three thousand years. The lotus flower is viewed as holy and elegant and is often praised in Chinese literature. It is a sacred flower in Buddhism too. Apart from its cultural significance and beauty, lotus is also delicious – all parts of the lotus plant are edible; the flower petals, seeds, young leaves and root can even be eaten raw. Many parts of the plant are also used in traditional herbal medicine and can be made into lotus tea, which is believed to be very healthy.

The part of the lotus that's consumed the most is definitely the root. Its mild yet refreshing sweetness and crunchy texture make it a very popular vegetable, often used in stir-fries, stews and soups. One of my favourite ways to cook it is with a sweet and sour sauce. The lotus root absorbs the flavourful sauce and softens after cooking but remains slightly crunchy.

糖醋藕丁

SWEET AND SOUR LOTUS ROOT

Soak the lotus root in cold water.

In a bowl, combine the soy sauce, dark vinegar, sugar and cornflour and mix well.

Heat a wok over a high heat and, once hot, add the oil and drained lotus. Pan-fry the lotus dice for about 5 minutes, stirring continuously to prevent burning, until they are golden and a bit crispy.

Push the lotus dice to one side of the wok and add the garlic to the other side. Stir for a little until you can smell the aroma of the garlic, then add the sauce. Reduce the heat to medium and keep stirring. Let it cook for about 3 minutes until most of the sauce has reduced, then finish with the spring onion.

350 g (12½ oz) lotus root, peeled and cut into 2 cm (¾ in) dice

2 tablespoons soy sauce

90 ml (3 fl oz) Chinese dark vinegar

1 tablespoon sugar

1½ teaspoons cornflour (cornstarch) or wheat starch

60 ml (2 fl oz/¼ cup) canola (rapeseed) oil

2 garlic cloves, roughly chopped

1 spring onion (scallion), sliced

This sour spicy lotus root is a very quick dish that requires very few ingredients. The lotus root is sour, spicy and crunchy, and it's perfect if you just want a small snack or light meal.

酸辣藕片

SOUR SPICY SLICED LOTUS ROOT

350 g (12½ oz) lotus root, peeled and ends trimmed

3 tablespoons canola (rapeseed) oil

3 garlic cloves, finely sliced

6 pickled chillies (see page 31)

75 ml (2½ fl oz) rice vinegar

½ teaspoon salt

1 spring onion (scallion), sliced

Slice the lotus root thinly and soak in cold water.

Heat a wok over a high heat and, once hot, add the oil and garlic and stir for 30 seconds. Add the pickled chilli, stir for 15 seconds, then add the drained lotus. Stir for 1–2 minutes until the lotus changes colour.

Add the rice vinegar, keep stirring for another 1–2 minutes, then add the salt and stir for 1 minute before adding the spring onion.

Kung Pao chicken is probably one of the most popular Chinese dishes overseas. Kung Pao is a cooking method from Sichuan that combines sweet and sour flavours with a slight spiciness from burnt dried chilli. The Kung Pao flavour is also described as a 'burnt spicy lychee flavour'. For this recipe I use king oyster mushroom as a substitute for chicken. It has a great texture and matches the other ingredients well.

宫保杏鲍菇

KUNG PAO KING OYSTER MUSHROOM

1 tablespoon soy sauce

1 teaspoon dark soy sauce

2 tablespoons Chinese dark vinegar

1 tablespoon Chinese cooking wine

1 tablespoon sugar

½ teaspoon salt

1 teaspoon cornflour (cornstarch) or potato starch

90 ml (3 fl oz) canola (rapeseed) oil

400 g (14 oz) king oyster mushrooms, cut into 1.5 cm (½ in) dice

3 garlic cloves, roughly chopped

50 g (1¾ oz) leek, finely sliced

10 dried chillies, destemmed and cut into short lengths

200 g (7 oz) cucumber, cut into 1.5 cm (½ in) dice

60 g (2 oz) roasted and salted peanuts

In a small bowl, combine the soy sauce, dark soy sauce, vinegar, cooking wine, sugar, salt and cornflour and mix well.

Heat a wok over a medium–high heat and, once hot, add 60 ml (2 fl oz/¼ cup) of the oil and the mushroom. Stir-fry for a few minutes until the mushroom dice shrink and some sides are a bit golden, then take them out.

Add the remaining oil to the wok with the garlic and leek and stir for 30 seconds. Add the dried chilli and stir-fry for another 30 seconds, then add the mushroom dice. Increase the heat to high and stir for 1 minute.

Add the sauce and stir until most of it has been absorbed by the mushrooms, then add the cucumber stir-frying for another minute. Add the peanuts, stir-frying for 15 seconds, then serve.

PREPARATION TIME
10 minutes

COOKING TIME
20 minutes

SERVES
2

This dish is so full of flavour. The oyster mushrooms are first dry-fried in oil, creating almost a jerky-like texture and taste, then they are stir-fried with the unique aroma of cumin and the spiciness of dried chilli.

乾煸孜然平菇

DRY-FRIED OYSTER MUSHROOMS WITH CUMIN

90 ml (3 fl oz) canola (rapeseed) oil

500 g (1 lb 2 oz) oyster mushrooms, hand pulled into strips

4 garlic cloves, roughly chopped

2 tablespoons cumin seeds

10 dried chillies, cut into short lengths

1 tablespoon Chilli oil (page 29)

2 tablespoons soy sauce

1 tablespoon vegan oyster sauce

1 spring onion (scallion), sliced

Heat a wok over a high heat and, once hot, add 60 ml (2 fl oz/¼ cup) of the oil and pan-fry the mushroom strips until brown and slightly crispy. Take them out.

Reduce the heat to medium–high and add the remaining oil with the garlic. Stir for 30 seconds, then add the cumin and dried chilli and stir for another 30 seconds. Add the chilli oil, stir for 15 seconds, then add the mushrooms.

Add the soy sauce and vegan oyster sauce and stir for 2–3 minutes until the sauce is absorbed by the mushrooms, then add the spring onion.

Hand-shredded cabbage is originally from Hunan and is one of the most popular vegetable dishes in Chinese cuisine. The special thing about this dish is that the cabbage is ripped by hand instead of cut by knife, because it's believed it tastes better this way. If you plan to cook several dishes for dinner, this one would be a great addition, and it's very easy and quick to make.

PREPARATION TIME
5 minutes

COOKING TIME
5 minutes

SERVES
2

手撕湾菜

HAND-SHREDDED CABBAGE

In a bowl, mix together the soy sauce, vinegar and sugar.

Heat a wok over a high heat and, once hot, add the oil and garlic and stir for 15 seconds, then add the dried chilli. Stir for another 15 seconds then add the cabbage and stir constantly for about 2–3 minutes until the cabbage changes colour.

Add the sauce and continue stirring for another 2–3 minutes until the cabbage absorbs the sauce and is cooked but still slightly crunchy. Don't overcook the cabbage, otherwise it gets soggy and watery.

3 tablespoons soy sauce

3 tablespoons Chinese dark vinegar

½ teaspoon sugar

60 ml (2 fl oz/¼ cup) canola (rapeseed) oil

3 garlic cloves, sliced

3 dried chillies, cut into short lengths

500 g (1 lb 2 oz) cabbage, hand-shredded into 3–4 cm (1¼–1½ in) pieces

Quick-fried Chinese cabbage with vinegar is originally from Shandong province. The Chinese cabbage is first fried in oil over a high heat, then cooked in a sour savoury sauce mixed with a bit of starch. This easy dish is always a good addition to the dinner table.

醋熘乞菜

QUICK-FRIED CHINESE CABBAGE WITH VINEGAR

60 ml (2 fl oz/¼ cup) rice vinegar

2 tablespoons soy sauce

⅔ teaspoon salt

1 teaspoon sugar

⅔ teaspoon cornflour (cornstarch) or potato starch

3 tablespoons canola (rapeseed) oil

4 garlic cloves, sliced

5 dried chillies, cut into short lengths

300 g (10½ oz) Chinese cabbage, cut into 3–4 cm (1¼–1½ in) pieces

1 tablespoon sesame oil

Mix the vinegar, soy sauce, salt, sugar and starch in a bowl.

Heat a wok over a high heat and, once hot, add the oil and garlic and stir for 15 seconds, then add the dried chilli. Stir for another 15 seconds, then add the cabbage and stir constantly for 1–2 minutes until the cabbage becomes soft.

Add the sauce and continue stirring for another 2–3 minutes. Add the sesame oil and stir for another 30 seconds before serving.

PREPARATION TIME
10 minutes

COOKING TIME
5 minutes

SERVES
2

Crunchy water spinach is a very popular vegetable in Chinese (especially Cantonese) and other South-East Asian cuisines. The easiest and most classic way to cook leafy greens is to stir-fry them with garlic, salt and soy sauce.

蒜蓉空心菜

STIR-FRIED WATER SPINACH

- 500 g (1 lb 2 oz) water spinach
- 3 tablespoons canola (rapeseed) oil
- 3 garlic cloves, roughly chopped
- 2 tablespoons soy sauce
- 1 tablespoon vegan oyster sauce

Wash and drain the water spinach, then cut it into 3 cm (1¼ in) lengths. Roughly separate the leaves from the stems, because the stems take a bit longer to cook.

Heat a wok over a high heat and, once hot, add the oil. Add the garlic and stir for about 30 seconds, then add the stems and stir for about 1 minute.

Add the leaves, stir quickly, then add the soy sauce and vegan oyster sauce. Stir for another minute until the water spinach is wilted.

Smacked cucumber salad is one of the most popular cold dishes in Chinese cuisine. To make this dish, the cucumber needs to be first smacked by the knife until it cracks, then cut into pieces, so it can absorb the seasoning better. With a few simple ingredients and 10 minutes of time, everyone can make this very refreshing salad at home.

PREPARATION TIME
10 minutes

SERVES
2

拍黄瓜

SMACKED CUCUMBER SALAD

Lay the cucumber on a work surface and smack it with the flat blade of a large knife until there are many cracks on the cucumber. Cut it into 4 cm (1½ in) lengths.

To a bowl, add the smacked cucumber, soy sauce, vinegar, chilli oil and chopped garlic.

Add the oil and sesame oil to a saucepan set over a medium–high heat and, when it is nice and hot (about 180°C/360°F), pour it on top of the cucumber salad. Mix well.

350 g (12½ oz) cucumber

1 tablespoon soy sauce

2 tablespoons Chinese dark vinegar

1 tablespoon chilli paste or oil (see page 29)

3 garlic cloves, finely chopped

2 tablespoons canola (rapeseed) oil

1 tablespoon sesame oil

PREPARATION TIME
10 minutes

COOKING TIME
20 minutes

SERVES
2

Taro is a root vegetable similar to yam. It is rich in starch and has a mild and slightly sweet taste. It can be made into savoury dishes or sweets or pastries. One of the most common ways of eating it is to simply steam it and dip it in sugar. In this recipe I red-braise the taro after pan-frying it a little. The taro is savoury, starchy and soaked with sauce after cooking.

红烧芋頭

RED-BRAISED TARO

500 g (1 lb 2 oz) taro

3 tablespoons canola (rapeseed) oil

3 garlic cloves, roughly chopped

5 dried chillies, cut into short lengths

3 tablespoons soy sauce

1 tablespoon dark soy sauce

1½ tablespoons vegan oyster sauce

180 (6 fl oz) hot water

1 spring onion (scallion), sliced

Peel the taro wearing kitchen gloves (as the slimy liquid of raw taro will make the skin itchy). Cut it into 3 cm (1¼ in) chunks.

Heat a wok over a medium heat and, once hot, add the oil. Add the taro and pan-fry for a few minutes until it's golden and crispy on the outside, then remove. Add the garlic, stir for 30 seconds, then add the dried chilli and stir for another 30 seconds.

Add the taro, soy sauce, dark soy sauce and vegan oyster sauce then add enough of the hot water to immerse most of the taro in the sauce. Let it cook for about 10 minutes until most of the sauce is gone, then add the spring onion.

Winter melon (also known as a 'wax melon') is a large fruit grown on a vine. It can reach 1 metre (3.3 feet) in length and weigh up to 50 kilograms (110 lb). It is normally harvested in late summer or autumn, but the waxy coating on a mature winter melon helps to preserve the melon over the colder months. When properly stored, it has a shelf life of a year or more without going bad. It's a great vegetable to have in summer, as it is believed to help with hydration and against heat strokes. Winter melon is very easy to cook, and this recipe is one of my favourite ways to cook it.

红烧冬瓜

RED-BRAISED WINTER MELON

800 g (1 lb 12 oz) winter melon (wax melon)

90 ml (3 fl oz) canola (rapeseed) oil

3 garlic cloves, roughly chopped

5 dried chillies, cut into short lengths

1 tablespoon fermented black beans

75 ml (2½ fl oz) soy sauce

1 tablespoon dark soy sauce

90 ml (3 fl oz) hot water

1 spring onion (scallion), sliced

Peel the winter melon and cut it into 4 cm (1½ in) chunks and score each cube every 5 mm (¼ in) without cutting it all the way through. This helps the winter melon to absorb the flavour.

Heat a wok over a medium heat and, once hot, add the oil. Add the winter melon and pan-fry for a few minutes until the top and bottom sides are golden, then take it out. Add the garlic and stir for 30 seconds, then add the dried chilli and fermented beans and stir for 30 seconds.

Return the winter melon to the wok along with the soy sauce and dark soy sauce. Then add enough of the hot water to immerse most of the winter melon in the sauce. Let it cook for 15 minutes, or until most of the sauce has reduced, then add the spring onion.

This is a very easy and yummy soup that can be made within a few minutes. The taste of tofu puffs and winter melon (wax melon) matches perfectly here and brings extra umami to the soup.

PREPARATION TIME
5 minutes

COOKING TIME
10 minutes

SERVES
2

冬瓜油豆腐湯

WINTER MELON SOUP WITH TOFU PUFFS

Heat a wok over a medium heat and, once hot, add the oil. Add the garlic and stir for 30 seconds, then add the winter melon and stir for 1–2 minutes until the winter melon becomes a little translucent and soft.

Add the hot water and bring to the boil, then add the tofu puffs and cook for 5 minutes, then add the salt and spring onion.

2 tablespoons canola (rapeseed) oil

3 garlic cloves, finely chopped

500 g (1 lb 2 oz) winter melon (wax melon), peeled and sliced

1 litre (34 fl oz/4 cups) hot water

100 g (3½ oz) fried tofu puffs, halved

½ teaspoon salt

1 spring onion (scallion), sliced

Dry pot is a unique method of cooking and serving from Sichuan. The dish is first cooked in the wok, then transferred to a tiny stainless-steel wok or 'dry pot'. A small flame is lit under the dry pot and the last part of the cooking is done in there at the table. Dry pot dishes have a special flavour and they are kept warm much longer than other stir-fried dishes because of the flame.

This cauliflower recipe is one of the most popular dry pot dishes. The best kind of cauliflower to use for this dish is called 'caulilini'. With long stems and loose curd, it has a crunchier and more refreshing taste than normal cauliflower, which is likely to become soggy after cooking in a sauce. If you want to try this dish but don't have a dry pot at home, you could simply stir-fry the onion together with the garlic and cook the cauliflower for 1–2 minutes longer in the wok after adding the sauces.

干鍋花菜

DRY POT CAULIFLOWER

½ onion, thinly sliced

90 ml (3 fl oz) canola (rapeseed) oil

400 g (14 oz) caulilini or cauliflower, broken into small pieces

3 garlic cloves, sliced

5 dried chillies, cut into pieces

2 tablespoons soy sauce

1 tablespoon vegan oyster sauce

1 teaspoon sugar

2 fresh chillies, destemmed and sliced

Put the onion in the dry pot.

Heat a wok over a high heat and, once hot, add 60 ml (2 fl oz/¼ cup) of the oil. Add the cauliflower and pan-fry for about 5 minutes until it's brown on the outside and almost cooked, then remove.

Add the remaining oil and the garlic and stir for 30 seconds, then add the dried chilli, stirring for another 30 seconds. Add the cauliflower and stir for about 1 minute, then add the soy sauce, vegan oyster sauce and sugar, stir for 2–3 minutes, then add the fresh chilli. Transfer everything to the dry pot with the onion and take it to the table. Allow the dish to continue cooking gently for a few minutes before serving.

PREPARATION TIME
5 minutes

COOKING TIME
10 minutes

SERVES
2

Oil-braised bamboo shoots are a traditional dish from the Jiangnan region of China, south of the lower reaches of the Yangtze River. The dish is made with fresh bamboo shoots, which have a very delicate earthy and nutty taste. In Jiangnan cuisine, it is believed that the fresher the ingredient is, the less seasoning it needs, so for this dish, only soy sauce, salt and sugar are used for seasoning.

油燜筍

OIL-BRAISED BAMBOO SHOOTS

300 g (10½ oz) bamboo shoots

1 teaspoon salt

15 g (½ oz) crystal sugar, crushed

90 ml (3 fl oz) canola (rapeseed) oil

3 tablespoons soy sauce

Peel the bamboo shoots and smack them a little with the knife, then cut them into 5 cm (2 in) lengths. Bring a saucepan of water to the boil and add the salt and bamboo shoots. Cook for 3 minutes, then take them out.

Heat a wok over a high heat and, once hot, add the oil. Add the bamboo shoots and pan-fry for a few minutes until they're slightly brown on the outside. Add the soy sauce, mix well and reduce the heat to medium–low. Put the lid on the wok and let it simmer for about 5 minutes.

Add the crystal sugar and stir until the sugar is completely dissolved then keep stirring until the sauce is about to be caramelised, then turn off the heat. Be careful not to cook the dish any longer, otherwise the sauce will burn.

ALL ABOUT NOODLES, DUMPLINGS AND RICE

There are a lot of differences between northern and southern Chinese diets. This is mainly dictated by the staple crops in each region. In the south, rice is the primary crop, and in the north it is wheat.

In most northern regions of China (except for the northeastern region), foods made with wheat flour make up a large part of the diet. There is an umbrella term, 麵食, for foods that are mainly made with wheat flour, such as noodles, dumplings, wonton, baozi, pancakes, steamed buns and bread. In some northern regions, such as Shanxi and Shaanxi, noodles form the main part of the daily diet. For example, Biang Biang noodles used to be the most common food for people in Shaanxi. In other northern regions, people would serve dishes with steamed bread or savoury pancakes. In the northeast, dumplings are the most beloved food.

Dumplings are very popular in the north in general. They are the festive food that families make and eat together on almost every traditional festival or important occasion, especially during Chinese New Year. In the south, making and eating dumplings at festivals is not a tradition, but it has also become increasingly popular in recent years.

There are three main ways to cook dumplings: boiling, steaming and pan-frying. In the north, the most common way to cook them is to boil them in water, and many people also drink some of the soup the dumplings were boiled in. In the south, dumplings are more commonly steamed and pan-fried than boiled. They are a popular street food and are often eaten as a snack on the run.

Noodles are also popular in the south, but many are not made with plain wheat like most noodle dishes from the north. In Sichuan and Hunan, noodle dishes made with alkaline noodles are popular. Egg noodles are also very popular in Cantonese cuisine, as are rice noodles, which are favoured in Hunan, Guangxi, Jiangxi and Yunnan.

Rice noodles were allegedly invented in ancient times by immigrants who travelled from the north to the south. They could not get used to rice instead of wheat noodles, so they created their own noodles made with rice instead. Hunan is best known for its rice noodles. Rice noodle dishes in this region are all made with fresh rice noodles, which have a better taste and texture than dried rice noodles. In the capital city, Changsha, flat rice noodles are the most popular kind, and in other parts of Hunan, round rice noodles are the only version of rice noodles. The rice used to make rice noodles is different to the rice that we eat on a regular basis. For example, to make Hunanese rice noodles, the best kind of rice is aged early-harvest long-grain rice (陳年早稻米).

In many southern regions, rice is planted twice a year. The first rice crops are normally planted in spring and harvested in mid-summer, and the growth cycle of the so-called early-harvest rice (早稻米) is normally 3–4 months. The second rice crops are called 'late-harvest rice' (晚稻米), which are planted in mid-summer and harvested in late autumn. The growth cycle is normally 4–5 months. The longer growth cycle determines that the quality and taste of late-harvest rice are better than those of early-harvest rice. Most of the rice varieties sold at supermarkets are late harvest. Early-harvest rice has a looser texture and a much lower transparency. It is less sticky and it absorbs more water. All of these traits make the early-harvest rice a poor rice option to eat directly, but ideal for making rice noodles.

Besides rice noodles, alkaline wheat noodles are also common in the south. The added alkali makes the noodles more elastic and prevents them from going sour. Most of the noodle dishes from Sichuan and Chongqing are made with alkaline wheat noodles, such as Chongqing xiao mian, Sichuan cold noodles and Yibin burning noodles. Alkaline wheat noodles are also popular in Hunan. At the local rice noodle restaurants, the alkaline wheat noodles are often the only alternative to rice noodles.

In most southern regions, a normal meal is several dishes served with rice, and southern dishes are typically smaller in portion than northern dishes. Besides plain rice, all kinds of fried rice are also very popular in the south. Fried rice can be a dish on its own when you don't feel like cooking anything else.

In Cantonese cuisine, congee is the most popular way to cook rice. Cantonese congee is typically plain and gently simmered for hours, then other ingredients and toppings are added. At Cantonese congee restaurants, there are normally dozens of different congee options, which can all be prepared within a few minutes, making it a very convenient quick meal.

In this chapter I will share many of my favourite noodle recipes, including plain wheat noodles, alkaline wheat noodles and rice noodles, as well as dumplings and rice dishes.

This noodle dish is also called Youpo mian (Oil spill noodles) or Kudai mian (Belt noodles). It is the most typical noodle dish from Shaanxi province, where they don't have access to a vast variety of different vegetables and crops compared to the south of China. Wheat has therefore always been the main crop and the base of the diet there. This dish used to be a typical peasant food in Shaanxi, because the ingredients are simple and cheap, and the carbs and oil provide enough calories for heavy physical labour in the fields.

Biang Biang noodles owes its name to the sound of the noodles being pulled and banged on the kitchen bench. The character 'biáng' (𰻞) is one of the most complex Chinese characters and is used specifically for this dish in modern Chinese. The noodles are also called 'belt noodles' owing to their length and thickness. They are chewier and more dense than the normal thin noodles.

PREPARATION TIME
1 hour

COOKING TIME
15 minutes

SERVES
2

油泼麺

BIANG BIANG NOODLES

In a large bowl, mix the flour with the salt and 200 ml (7 fl oz) water (use lukewarm water in winter and room-temperature water in summer). Cover the bowl with a damp cloth and let it rest for 10 minutes. This step will help the ingredients bind together and, therefore, reduce the kneading time.

Knead the dough until it's more or less smooth then return it to the bowl and cover with a damp cloth again. Rest for 30 minutes.

Knead the dough again for a few minutes until it's smooth. Cut the dough into six equal pieces, then use a rolling pin to roll out each piece to create 20 cm (8 in) lengths. Working with one noodle at a time, take an end in each hand and carefully stretch it longer while banging it on a clean kitchen bench until you have a long, belt-shaped noodle about 3 mm (⅛ in) thick.

Bring a large pot of water to the boil and add the noodles. Stir occasionally until they are cooked – this should take 8–12 minutes depending on the size and thickness of your noodles. To test if they are done, cut a noodle in half. If the centre is still hard and white, it needs a bit longer, but be careful not to overcook the noodles, otherwise they become soggy.

400 g (14 oz/2⅔ cups) plain (all-purpose) flour

1 teaspoon salt

60 ml (2 fl oz/¼ cup) soy sauce

90 ml (3 fl oz) Chinese dark vinegar

6 garlic cloves, finely chopped

25 g (1 oz) chilli flakes

2 spring onions (scallions), finely chopped

90 ml (3 fl oz) canola (rapeseed) oil

Drain the water and divide the noodles equally between two big bowls. Add half of the soy sauce, dark vinegar, garlic, chilli flakes and spring onion to each bowl.

Heat the oil in a saucepan over a high heat until it's very hot (when it starts to smoke a little bit), then pour the hot oil over the noodles. Mix everything well before eating.

PREPARATION TIME
15 minutes

COOKING TIME
10 minutes

SERVES
2

Sichuan cold noodles is a very popular dish from Sichuan. The noodles being cold, elastic and flavourful makes them a delightful treat in summer. This dish is originally made with fresh alkaline wheat noodles – the added alkali makes the noodles slightly yellow and more elastic. You can also use dried alkaline noodles if you can't find the fresh ones.

四川涼麺

SICHUAN COLD NOODLES

2 garlic cloves, finely chopped

10 g (¼ oz) piece of fresh ginger, finely chopped

100 g (3½ oz) bean sprouts

300 g (10½ oz) fresh alkaline wheat noodles, or 200 g (7 oz) dried

2 tablespoons soy sauce

60 ml (2 fl oz/¼ cup) sesame oil

2 tablespoons Chinese dark vinegar

2 tablespoons Chilli oil (page 29)

2 teaspoons sugar

½ teaspoon ground sichuan peppercorns

2 spring onions (scallions), sliced

Put the garlic in a bowl with 2 tablespoons water, and put the ginger in a separate bowl with 2 tablespoons water.

Bring a saucepan of water to the boil and blanch the bean sprouts for 15 seconds. Remove and divide between two serving bowls.

Cook the noodles until they are al dente (the core of the noodle should still be a little bit white), being very careful not to overcook them. Take them out when they are still elastic and drain well. Transfer the noodles to a baking sheet or a flat kitchen surface and add the sesame oil. Mix it well with the noodles so they don't stick together then toss the noodles with chopsticks to help them cool down quickly.

After the noodles have cooled down, divide them equally between the two bowls. Divide the remaining ingredients between the two serving bowls and mix everything together well before eating.

Zha jiang mian means 'fried sauce noodles' in Chinese. It is the most traditional and popular noodle dish from Beijing. It typically consists of thick wheat noodles topped with zhajiang sauce, bean sprouts and cucumber strips. Zhajiang sauce is normally made with minced (ground) meat, sweet bean sauce (甜麵醬) and soybean paste (黄豆酱). In this recipe I have used vegan mince and smoked tofu to add some extra flavour.

炸醬麵

ZHA JIANG MIAN

90 ml (3 fl oz) canola (rapeseed) oil

2 garlic cloves, chopped

30 g (1 oz) leek, finely chopped

10 g (¼ oz) piece of fresh ginger, finely chopped

100 g (3½ oz) vegan mince

200 g (7 oz) smoked tofu, cut into small dice

3 tablespoons Tianmian (sweet bean) sauce (page 34)

80 g (2¾ oz) soybean paste

90 ml (3 fl oz) hot water

100 g (3½ oz) bean sprouts

450 g (1 lb) fresh thick wheat noodles, or 300 g (10½ oz) dried

½ cucumber, cut into thin strips

1 spring onion (scallion), sliced

Heat a wok over a medium heat and, once hot, add the oil. Add the garlic, leek and ginger, and stir for 30 seconds. Add the vegan mince and use a spatula to break it into small pieces. Stir-fry for 2–3 minutes until it changes colour, then add the smoked tofu and stir for 1 minute.

Add the sweet bean sauce, soybean paste and hot water, and let the sauce simmer for about 10 minutes, stirring occasionally to make sure it doesn't stick to the wok.

Bring a saucepan of water to the boil and blanch the bean sprouts for 30 seconds, then remove. Add the noodles and cook until they are al dente.

Dress the noodles with the zhajiang sauce and top with the bean sprouts, cucumber strips and spring onion.

Cold-braised rice noodles are quite popular in many southern parts of China, especially during summer, and every region has its own version. The noodles are first cooked then mixed with sauces, seasonings and toppings. It's a simple dish, but it's full of flavour.

Zhacai, or Tsa tsai, is pickled mustard plant stem, which is normally served as a side dish or as a topping for congee and noodles, but it can also be used in cooking, for example in fried rice, fried noodles or this recipe. Zhacai can be found in any Asian grocery store and is usually sold in small packages.

PREPARATION TIME
30 minutes

COOKING TIME
15 minutes

SERVES
2

涼拌粉

COLD-BRAISED RICE NOODLES

Cook the rice noodles for 2 minutes less than the packet instructions advise, then drain and soak in cold water. Be careful not to overcook the noodles.

Heat a saucepan over a medium heat and, once hot, add the sesame oil and garlic. Stir for a little until the garlic becomes fragrant, then add the sesame seeds, bird's eye chilli and five spice and stir for 30 seconds. Add the soy sauce and vegan oyster sauce. When the sauce starts to boil, divide equally between two bowls.

Bring another saucepan of water to the boil and cook the rice noodles for about 30 seconds, to the point where they are exactly al dente and very elastic. Drain and distribute them evenly between the two bowls.

Divide the remaining ingredients between the bowls and serve.

500 g (1 lb 2 oz) fresh rice noodles, or 300 g (10½ oz) dried rice noodles

3 tablespoons sesame oil

3 garlic cloves, finely chopped

1 teaspoon toasted sesame seeds

2 bird's eye chillies, destemmed and chopped

½ teaspoon five spice (see page 27)

60 ml (2 fl oz/¼ cup) soy sauce

3 tablespoons vegan oyster sauce

2 tablespoons Chinese dark vinegar

2 tablespoons Chilli oil (page 29)

60 g (2 oz) Zhacai or Tsa tsai, chopped

½ cucumber, cut into thin strips

60 g (2 oz) fried or roasted peanuts

2 spring onions (scallions), sliced

1 coriander (cilantro) sprig, roughly chopped

PREPARATION TIME
30 minutes

COOKING TIME
15 minutes

SERVES
2

Little pot rice noodles is originally from Yunnan. The dish has this name because the authentic way to cook it is in a small copper pot. At restaurants, each pot of noodles is served to the customer as one portion. It is best to use fresh rice noodles, which reduces the cooking time substantially, but you can also use the dried ones.

The rice noodles are normally cooked in a soup with pickled mustard greens (酸腌菜), garlic chives and minced (ground) pork. Here we use vegan mince instead. This one-pot dish is the perfect comfort food for a cold day. It's also a great go-to option if you are only cooking for yourself.

500 g (1 lb 2 oz) fresh rice noodles, or 300 g (10½ oz) dried rice noodles

60 ml (2 fl oz/¼ cup) canola (rapeseed) oil

6 garlic cloves, roughly chopped

10 g (¼ oz) piece of fresh ginger, chopped

200 g (7 oz) tomatoes, diced

200 g (7 oz) pickled mustard greens, chopped

1 litre (34 fl oz/4 cups) hot water

200 g (7 oz) vegan mince

3 tablespoons soy sauce

1 tablespoon dark soy sauce

2 tablespoons vegan oyster sauce

1 teaspoon salt

100 g (3½ oz) garlic chives, cut into pieces

2 tablespoons Chilli oil (page 29)

1 spring onion (scallion), cut into 3 cm (1¼ in) lengths

小鍋米線

LITTLE POT RICE NOODLES

If you are using dried rice noodles, fill a saucepan with cold water and add the noodles. Place over a medium–high heat and cook for 2 minutes less than what the packet instructions advise, stirring so the noodles don't stick together. The noodles are ready when they are almost al dente but the core of the noodles is still a little hard. Be very careful not to overcook the noodles because they need to be cooked again later. Drain and immediately soak the noodles in iced water to stop the cooking process. If you use fresh rice noodles you can skip this step.

Heat a small saucepan over a medium heat. Add the oil, garlic and ginger and stir for about 30 seconds until the aromas come out, then add the tomato and stir for 1–2 minutes until it is soft and cooked. Add the pickled mustard greens and stir for another minute.

Add the hot water and, once it is boiling, add the vegan mince, soy sauce, dark soy sauce, vegan oyster sauce and salt.

Add the rice noodles and cook for 1 minute then turn off the heat and add the garlic chives, chilli oil and spring onion.

In this recipe, the rice noodles are first cooked then stir-fried together with different ingredients. Check to see if you can find sword beans at your local Asian grocer, but if not, runner beans work just as well for this recipe. You can also add any other ingredients you like.

炒粿

STIR-FRIED RICE NOODLES

350 g (12½ oz) fresh rice noodles, or 200 g (7 oz) dried rice noodles

120 ml (4 fl oz) canola (rapeseed) oil

200 g (7 oz) tender or firm tofu, cut into strips

6 sword or runner beans, cut into 3 cm (1¼ in) lengths

100 g (3½ oz) tinned bamboo shoots, drained and cut into thin strips

2 shallots, thinly sliced

100 g (3½ oz) light-green zucchini (courgette), cut into thin strips

5 shiitake mushrooms, soaked for 2 hours then cut into thin strips

5 g (⅛ oz) wood ear mushrooms, soaked for 30 minutes then cut into thin strips

2 tablespoons hoisin sauce

1 tablespoon soy sauce

2 tablespoons vegan oyster sauce

1 tablespoon toasted sesame seeds

1 spring onion (scallion), cut into pieces

Bring a saucepan of water to the boil and cook the rice noodles until almost al dente (about 2 minutes less than the packet instructs), then pour them into a sieve and run them under cold water to wash off the starch. Drain, then soak them in fresh cold water. Be careful not to overcook the noodles, otherwise they will start to break while stir-frying.

Heat a wok over a medium–high heat and, once hot, add half of the oil and pan-fry the tofu until both sides are golden and crispy, then take it out.

Add the remaining oil and increase the heat to high. Add the sword beans and stir for 1 minute, then add the bamboo shoots and stir for another minute. Add the shallot and stir for 30 seconds, then add the zucchini and stir for another 30 seconds. Add the shiitake and wood ear mushrooms and stir for 1 minute.

Add the rice noodles and tofu and stir everything together. Add the hoisin sauce, soy sauce and vegan oyster sauce and mix everything together well, stirring for another 2–3 minutes until the sauce has been fully absorbed by the noodles. Add the sesame and spring onion.

Liang pi literally means 'cold skin' in Chinese. It is a famous street food from Shaanxi province. Although it might look like wide rice noodles, there is no rice involved. Instead, plain (all-purpose) wheat flour is kneaded into dough, then washed over and over again until the wheat starch has been washed out. The concentrated starchy mixture is then steamed quickly on a flat plate and cut into noodles. The remaining part of the washed dough is natural gluten, which is normally mixed with yeast and steamed as well to be used as a topping for liang pi. But since that traditional method is very time consuming, I have simplified this recipe using a steamed batter.

PREPARATION TIME
15 minutes

COOKING TIME
30 minutes

SERVES
2

涼皮

LIANG PI (COLD-SKIN NOODLES)

In a big bowl, mix the flour, starch, salt and 750 ml (25½ fl oz/3 cups) water. Filter the batter with a sieve to remove any small lumps, as these will cause your skin noodles to be lumpy after steaming.

Soak the garlic in 60 ml (2 fl oz/¼ cup) water, while you complete the other steps.

Brush a little of the sesame oil over a flat plate – preferably stainless steel, but any flat plate will do. Mix the batter again and pour a thin layer of it onto the plate.

Fill a saucepan with hot water and place a steam rack in the pot (the water level should not be higher than the steam rack). Place the plate on top of the steam rack, cover with a lid and let it steam over a high heat for 3–5 minutes. (The exact time will depend on how thick your layer is and how thick the plate is.)

When the noodle sheet has become completely translucent, carefully take the plate out. Fill a large bowl or container with cold water and float the plate in the water to help it cool down. Once cool enough to handle, remove the noodle sheet carefully. Set it aside and brush with a thin layer of sesame oil to prevent it sticking and drying. Repeat this step until all of the batter has been steamed.

Slice the noodles into 1 cm (½ in) thick strips and divide them between two bowls.

Divide the garlic and its water, chilli oil, sesame paste, soy sauce, dark vinegar, cucumber, peanuts and spring onion between the bowls. Mix everything well before eating.

150 g (5½ oz/1 cup) plain (all-purpose) flour

250 g (9 oz) wheat starch

1 teaspoon salt

5 garlic cloves, finely chopped

60 ml (2 fl oz/¼ cup) sesame oil

60 ml (2 fl oz/¼ cup) Chilli oil (page 29)

60 g (2 oz) Sesame paste/sauce (page 49)

2 tablespoons soy sauce

2 tablespoons Chinese dark vinegar

½ cucumber, cut into thin strips

60 g (2 oz) fried or roasted peanuts

2 spring onions (scallions), sliced

Hot dry noodles is a famous noodle from Wuhan, most typically eaten as breakfast. For hot dry noodles, fresh alkaline wheat noodles are first cooked until almost al dente, then cooled down with a ventilator or hand-held fan and coated in sesame oil to avoid them sticking together. Before serving, the noodles are cooked again quickly then topped with sesame paste, pickled radish and other seasonings.

熱乾麵

HOT DRY NOODLES

4 garlic cloves, finely chopped

300 g (10½ oz) fresh alkaline wheat noodles, or 200 g (7 oz) dried alkaline wheat noodles

120 ml (4 fl oz) sesame oil

3 tablespoons light soy sauce

2 teaspoons dark soy sauce

90 ml (3 fl oz) Sesame paste/ sauce (page 49)

60 ml (2 fl oz/¼ cup) Chilli oil (page 29)

100 g (3½ oz) pickled spicy radish, chopped

2 spring onions (scallions), sliced

1 coriander (cilantro) sprig, chopped

Mix the garlic in a bowl with 90 ml (3 fl oz) water.

Bring a saucepan of water to the boil and cook the noodles until they are almost al dente (when the core is still a bit white). Be careful not to overcook the noodles. Drain when they are still elastic.

Tip the noodles onto a big plate or clean kitchen bench and add 90 ml (3 fl oz) of the sesame oil, tossing the noodles in the oil constantly to cool them down and prevent them from sticking together. (It's even better to have a ventilator or hand-held fan blowing the noodles from the side.) These noodles can be kept aside for a few hours. Just cover them with a slightly damp cloth if you plan to use them within a few hours.

Bring a saucepan of water to the boil and add the noodles. Cook for 15 seconds then drain the water and divide the noodles evenly between two bowls.

Divide the garlic and its water, the remaining sesame oil, light soy sauce, dark soy sauce, sesame paste and chilli oil evenly between the bowls. Top with some pickled radish, spring onion and coriander. Mix everything well before eating.

Yibin burning noodles is a famous dish from the city of Yibin, Sichuan. As in many other Sichuan noodle dishes, fresh alkaline noodles are used here. The noodles are first cooked until they are almost al dente, then mixed with chilli oil and other ingredients. They are called 'burning noodles' because, theoretically, you could light the noodles on fire, since they are covered with oil and dry ingredients. Sichuan preserved leaf mustard can be found in most Asian grocery stores.

宜賓燃麺

YIBIN BURNING NOODLES

1 tablespoon canola (rapeseed) oil

60 g (2 oz) Sichuan preserved leaf mustard

300 g (10½ oz) fresh alkaline wheat noodles, or 200 g (7 oz) dried alkaline wheat noodles

2 garlic cloves, finely chopped

60 ml (2 fl oz/¼ cup) soy sauce

2 tablespoons sesame oil

90 ml (3 fl oz) Chilli oil (page 29)

35 g (1¼ oz) roasted and salted peanuts, crushed

2 tablespoons toasted sesame seeds

2 spring onions (scallions), sliced

coriander (cilantro) leaves, to garnish

Heat a small, non-stick frying pan over a medium heat and, once hot, add the oil and Sichuan preserved mustard. Stir-fry for about 1 minute, then set aside for later.

Bring a saucepan of water to the boil and cook the noodles until they are al dente (when the core of the noodle is still a little bit white). Be careful not to overcook the noodles – when they are still elastic, drain well.

Divide the noodles and preserved mustard evenly between two bowls along with the remaining ingredients. Mix everything well before eating.

Xiao mian is a spicy noodle dish from the city of Chongqing, although it has become a very popular food all over China in the last few years. It literally means 'little noodles' in Chinese. Xiao mian can be served with or without toppings. Here, we have the recipes for two toppings for xiao mian: zajiang and smashed yellow pea.

PREPARATION TIME
8½ hours

COOKING TIME
2 hours

SERVES
2

小麺

XIAO MIAN (CHONGQING NOODLES)

Start by making the smashed yellow peas. Soak the peas in water with the soda ash overnight. Drain the water, then add the peas to a pot with the ginger and salt. Fill with the hot water and let it cook over a medium–high heat for 2 hours, topping up the water as necessary. If you have a pressure cooker, you can cook the beans in there instead and they will only take about 15 minutes to cook.

The peas are ready when they are a little mushy but not completely soft. Drain the water and discard the ginger. Add the cooked peas to a bowl and set aside.

To make the zajiang topping, heat a wok over a medium heat and, once hot, add the oil and vegan mince. Break the mince into small pieces with a spatula and stir-fry for 3–5 minutes until it's brown and a bit crispy on the outside.

Add the garlic and ginger and stir-fry for 15 seconds. Add the Pixian broad bean paste and stir-fry for 30 seconds then add the sweet bean paste and stir-fry for 1 minute.

Add the soy sauce and dark soy sauce and stir-fry for 30 seconds. Add the warm water and cooking wine, reduce the heat to low and simmer for 5–10 minutes until most of the sauce is reduced. Turn off the heat.

Smashed yellow pea topping

100 g (3½ oz) dried yellow or white peas

½ teaspoon soda ash (sodium carbonate)

10 g (¼ oz) piece of fresh ginger, thinly sliced

1 teaspoon salt

2 litres (68 fl oz/8 cups) hot water

Zajiang topping

60 ml (2 fl oz/¼ cup) canola (rapeseed) oil

200 g (7 oz) vegan mince

3 garlic cloves, chopped

10 g (¼ oz) piece of fresh ginger, finely chopped

1 tablespoon Pixian broad bean paste (see page 26)

1 tablespoon sweet bean paste

1 tablespoon soy sauce

1 teaspoon dark soy sauce

90 ml (3 fl oz) warm water

60 ml (2 fl oz/¼ cup) Chinese cooking wine

Xiao mian

3 garlic cloves, finely chopped

10 g (¼ oz) piece of fresh ginger, finely chopped

700 ml (23½ fl oz) vegetable stock

½ teaspoon ground sichuan peppercorns

¼ teaspoon salt

60 ml (2 fl oz/¼ cup) red soy sauce

1 tablespoon sesame oil

1 tablespoon Chinese dark vinegar

1 tablespoon Sesame paste/ sauce (page 49)

60 ml (2 fl oz/¼ cup) Chilli oil (page 29)

300 g (10½ oz) fresh alkaline wheat noodles, or 200 g (7 oz) dried alkaline wheat noodles

180 g (6½ oz) Zajiang topping (see opposite)

150 g (5½ oz) Smashed yellow peas (see opposite)

2 tablespoons Sichuan preserved leaf mustard (found at most Asian/Chinese stores)

2 tablespoons roasted and salted peanuts, crushed

1 spring onion (scallion), sliced

1 coriander (cilantro) sprig, chopped

To make the xiao mian, add the chopped garlic and ginger to a small bowl with 90 ml (3 fl oz) water. Bring the vegetable stock to the boil in a saucepan.

Divide the ground peppercorn, salt, red soy sauce, sesame oil, dark vinegar, sesame paste and chilli oil between two bowls. Divide the garlic and ginger and their soaking water evenly between the bowls, followed by the vegetable stock.

Cook the noodles according to the packet instructions until they are al dente, then divide them equally between the two bowls.

To each bowl of noodles, add half of the zajiang and half of the smashed yellow peas, 1 tablespoon preserved mustard and 1 tablespoon crushed peanuts, then sprinkle the spring onion and coriander on top.

Any leftover zajiang or smashed peas can be stored in an airtight container in the fridge for up to 3 days. Both toppings are great on congee and noodle dishes.

PREPARATION TIME
45 minutes

COOKING TIME
15 minutes

SERVES
2

Tianshui noodles are a famous street food from Chengdu. Tianshui literally means 'sweet water' in Chinese. The noodles are very thick and chewy, spicy, savoury and also sweet at the same time.

甜水麵

TIANSHUI MIAN (SWEET SICHUAN NOODLES)

300 g (10½ oz/1⅓ cups) plain (all-purpose) flour, plus extra for dusting

½ teaspoon salt

½ teaspoon five spice (see page 27)

60 ml (2 fl oz/¼ cup) red soy sauce

2 tablespoons sesame oil

2 tablespoons Chilli oil (page 29)

1 tablespoon Sesame paste/sauce (page 49)

2 garlic cloves, finely chopped

3 tablespoons salted and roasted peanuts, crushed

In a big bowl, mix the flour and salt together with 140 ml (4½ fl oz) water. Knead it into a smooth dough. Shape it into a ball and cover with a damp cloth. Let it rest for 30 minutes.

Sprinkle some flour on your clean kitchen bench. First, press the dough flat with your palm, then use a rolling pin to roll it into a rectangle about 5 mm (¼ in) thick. Sprinkle some more flour on top.

Fold the flat dough so it's easier to cut, then use a sharp knife to cut the noodles out (each noodle should be about 1 cm/½ in wide). Working with one noodle at a time, take an end in each hand and stretch it slightly longer.

Bring a saucepan of water to the boil and cook the noodles until they are al dente, about 6–8 minutes depending on the thickness of the noodles. Stir gently with chopsticks so they don't stick to the pot. Drain and divide between two bowls.

Divide the remaining ingredients between the two bowls and mix everything together well.

Spring onion (scallion) oil noodles is a typical dish from Shanghai and its surrounding regions. Fresh spring onion is fried in oil over a low heat to slowly extract the flavour. Once you have the spring onion oil, the only thing you have to do is boil noodles and mix it in. It's incredibly simple and flavourful. The fragrant oil can be used in other dishes to enhance the flavour – it will keep in the fridge for up to 3 months.

PREPARATION TIME
10 minutes

COOKING TIME
30 minutes

SERVES
2

SPRING ONION OIL NOODLES

Cut eight spring onions into 3 cm (1¼ in) pieces and separate the white parts (stems) and the green parts (leaves). Finely slice the other two spring onions for the noodles later.

Heat a small saucepan over a medium heat and add the oil. When the oil is hot, add the whites of the spring onions and the red shallot and reduce the heat to medium–low.

When the spring onion and shallot are turning a little brown, add the greens of the spring onions and turn the heat to low. Let it fry until everything is brown, then switch off the heat. Allow to cool then filter the oil through a sieve into a bowl, reserving some of the fried onion and shallots to serve.

Bring a saucepan of water to the boil and cook the noodles according to the packet instructions until they are al dente. Meanwhile, to another saucepan add 90 ml (3 fl oz) of the spring onion oil, the soy sauce and dark soy sauce. When the sauce boils, divide it equally between two bowls.

When the noodles are al dente, divide them between the bowls, then add the cut fresh spring onion and some of the fried onion and shallots as toppings. Mix everything well before eating.

10 spring onions (scallions)
240 ml (8 fl oz) canola (rapeseed) oil
3 red shallots, sliced
300 g (10½ oz) fresh thin wheat noodles, or 200 g (7 oz) dried thin wheat noodles
60 ml (2 fl oz/¼ cup) soy sauce
2 tablespoons dark soy sauce

PREPARATION TIME
30 minutes

COOKING TIME
5 minutes

SERVES
2

Beef chow fun is a staple Cantonese dish and best represents the concept of Wok Hei (see page 19). Chow fun means 'fried rice noodles' in Cantonese, and it is traditionally made with beef. Here, I use king oyster mushrooms instead. The best kind of rice noodles for this dish are fresh shahe fen (沙河粉), but dried rice noodles can also be used in their place. This is a dish that I grew up eating as it is sold everywhere in Guangzhou, in restaurants and at food stands.

素乾炒菇河

MUSHROOM CHOW FUN

300 g (10½ oz) fresh wide rice noodles, or 200 g (7 oz) dried wide rice noodles

60 ml (2 fl oz/¼ cup) soy sauce

2 tablespoons vegan oyster sauce

½ teaspoon salt

3 king oyster mushrooms, thinly sliced

1 tablespoon dark soy sauce

1 teaspoon sugar

120 ml (4 fl oz) canola (rapeseed) oil

1 red shallot, thinly sliced

2 garlic cloves, chopped

100 g (3½ oz) bean sprouts

100 g (3½ oz) yellow or green Chinese chives, cut into 3 cm (1¼ in) lengths

1 spring onion (scallion), cut into 3 cm (1¼ in) lengths

If you are using dried noodles, soak them first in lukewarm water for 30 minutes.

Combine 1 tablespoon of the soy sauce, 1 tablespoon of the vegan oyster sauce and the salt in a bowl and add the mushrooms. Leave to marinate for 15 minutes.

In another bowl, mix together the remaining soy sauce and vegan oyster sauce, the dark soy sauce and the sugar.

Heat a wok over a medium–high heat and, once hot, add half of the oil. Drain any marinade that the mushrooms have not absorbed and add the mushroom to the wok. Pan-fry until a bit brown and cooked on both sides, then remove.

Switch to the highest heat and add the rest of the oil, the shallot and garlic and stir-fry for 15 seconds. Add the mushroom slices and stir for 15 seconds, then add the drained noodles and stir for 30 seconds to 1 minute until the noodles are a bit softer. Then add the sauce, using chopsticks to quickly mix everything together. Toss the wok and stir constantly, being careful not to break the noodles.

When the noodles are almost cooked, add the bean sprouts and stir-fry for 15–30 seconds then add the garlic chives and stir-fry for another 15–30 seconds. Finish with the spring onion and serve.

Hong Kong supreme soy sauce fried noodles is one of the most popular noodle dishes in Cantonese cuisine. The traditional version is vegetarian, and it is typically made with egg noodles, bean sprouts, shallots, yellow garlic chives and a mixed sauce. For this recipe I use dried noodles made for frying, for example, instant noodles. They are elastic and slightly chewy, similar to egg noodles.

豉油皇炒麵

HONG KONG SUPREME SOY SAUCE FRIED NOODLES

200 g (7 oz) dried noodles for frying

2 tablespoons soy sauce or light soy sauce

3 tablespoons dark soy sauce

1 tablespoon vegan oyster sauce

1 teaspoon sugar

120 ml (4 fl oz) canola (rapeseed) oil

1 red shallot, thinly sliced

1 garlic clove, chopped

100 g (3½ oz) bean sprouts

50 g (1¾ oz) garlic chives, cut into 3 cm (1¼ in) lengths

1 spring onion (scallion), cut into 3 cm (1¼ in) lengths

Bring a saucepan of water to the boil then turn off the heat. Add the noodles and let them soak in the hot water for 1–2 minutes until they are loose and half-cooked (it depends on which noodles you are using; the soaking may take longer). Do not soak for too long, otherwise the noodles will become soggy later. Drain the water and blow the noodles dry with a ventilator or hand-held fan.

Mix the soy sauce, dark soy sauce, vegan oyster sauce and sugar in a small bowl together.

Heat a wok over a medium heat and, once hot, add half of the oil then add the noodles. Slowly pan-fry until the outside of the noodles is a bit golden and crispy, about 2–3 minutes, then take them out.

Switch to the highest heat, add the rest of the oil, the shallot and garlic and stir-fry for 15 seconds, then add the noodles and stir-fry for 30 seconds. Add the mixed sauce and use chopsticks to quickly mix everything together, being careful not to break the noodles.

Stir-fry for 1–2 minutes, and when the noodles are cooked and the sauce has been absorbed, add the bean sprouts and stir-fry for 15 seconds. Add the garlic chives and stir-fry for another 15 seconds before adding the spring onion and cooking for another 30 seconds.

Plain noodles is a simple dish from the Jiangnan region. It is called 'plain' noodles because it is served in a clear soup without any topping. Traditionally, the noodles are first cooked then served in a soup seasoned with mainly soy sauce and lard. Here, I use sesame oil instead. It is a very quick and simple dish, especially if you are feeling like eating noodles for dinner but don't have many ingredients at home or much time to cook.

陽春麵

PLAIN NOODLES

720 ml (24½ fl oz) vegetable stock

2 tablespoons sesame oil

90 ml (3 fl oz) soy sauce or light soy sauce

1 tablespoon dark soy sauce

½ teaspoon salt

½ teaspoon sugar

300 g (10½ oz) fresh thin wheat noodles, or 200 g (7 oz) dried thin wheat noodles

1 spring onion (scallion), sliced

Bring the vegetable stock to the boil in a saucepan.

Divide the sesame oil, soy sauce, dark soy sauce, salt, sugar and veggie stock between two bowls.

Bring another saucepan of water to the boil and cook the noodles according to the packet instructions. Divide them evenly between the two bowls then top with the spring onion.

PREPARATION TIME
5 minutes

COOKING TIME
5 minutes

SERVES
2

Soy sauce fried rice is one of the simplest and most classic fried rice recipes: it's super easy and quick to make and it requires so few ingredients. If you have some leftover cooked rice at home – ideally from the night before – and don't know what to make for dinner, then try this.

醬油炒飯

SOY SAUCE FRIED RICE

90 ml (3 fl oz) canola (rapeseed) oil

500 g (1 lb 2 oz) leftover cooked long-grain rice

½ onion, diced

80 g (2¾ oz) pickled mustard or Tsa tsai, cut into pieces

3 tablespoons soy sauce

1 tablespoon dark soy sauce

1 tablespoon vegan oyster sauce

1 spring onion (scallion), sliced

Heat a wok over a medium–high heat and, once hot, add 3 tablespoons of the oil. Add the leftover rice, loosening it up with a spatula, and fry until it's a little dry, loose and browned on the outside. Remove the rice and set aside.

Add the remaining oil and the onion and stir for 30 seconds, then add the pickled mustard and stir for another 30 seconds. Turn the heat to high and add the rice. Stir for a little, then add the soy sauce, dark soy sauce and vegan oyster sauce. Stir well to ensure the rice is evenly coated.

Continue stirring for another 1–2 minutes until the rice is not soggy anymore and has completely absorbed the sauce, then add the spring onion and turn off the heat.

Congee is basically rice porridge, and it is quite a common dish in many Asian countries, but the making of it differs from place to place. Cantonese congee is the most famous and popular version in China. There is a plain congee (白粥), and there are also many congee dishes cooked with different ingredients; among the most famous are Sampan congee, fish congee and congee with hundred-year egg and pork.

In Cantonese food culture, congee is eaten at breakfast, lunch and dinner and even as a late-night snack. Congee (especially plain congee) is regarded as the perfect food for the sick, for example when you have a stomach problem. It is easy to digest and soothes and warms the stomach without adding too much burden to it. Congee can be eaten with many side dishes. Some of my favourites are fried peanuts, preserved olives and spicy fermented tofu.

青菜粥
PAK CHOI CONGEE

Rinse the rice then add it to a clay pot (or a normal pot). Add the salt and oil, mix everything together and leave the rice to marinate for 30 minutes. This step helps the rice cook more quickly and smoothly later.

Add the hot water and bring it to the boil, stirring occasionally. Add the salted radish and shiitake and let it cook over a medium–low heat for 1 hour, stirring regularly to prevent sticking.

When the congee is thick and smooth, add salt to taste, followed by the pak choi. Stir and let it cook for another 30 seconds, then add the spring onion and serve with your choice of side dishes.

100 g (3½ oz/½ cup) white rice

½ teaspoon salt, plus more to taste

1 tablespoon canola (rapeseed) oil

1.5 litres (51 fl oz/6 cups) hot water

100 g (3½ oz) salted radish or preserved turnip, cut into pieces

100 g (3½ oz) fresh shiitake mushrooms, thinly sliced, or 20 g (¾ oz) dried shiitake mushrooms, soaked for 2 hours then sliced thinly

2 pak choi, cut into pieces

1 spring onion (scallion), sliced

PREPARATION TIME
5 minutes

COOKING TIME
5 minutes

SERVES
2

Wontons in chilli oil are a popular street food from Sichuan. These wontons have a thinner wrap and are, in general, smaller than normal dumplings. They are first cooked and then served with a spicy sauce made with chilli oil and other seasonings.

红油抄手

WONTONS IN CHILLI OIL

2 garlic cloves, finely chopped

60 ml (2 fl oz/¼ cup) Chilli oil (page 29)

2 tablespoons sesame oil

60 ml (2 fl oz/¼ cup) soy sauce

1 tablespoon dark soy sauce

2 tablespoons Chinese dark vinegar

1 tablespoon toasted sesame seeds

40 vegan wontons

2 spring onions (scallions), sliced

Divide the garlic, chilli oil, sesame oil, soy sauce, dark soy sauce, dark vinegar and toasted sesame between two bowls.

Bring a saucepan of water to the boil and add the wontons. Stir occasionally so that the wontons don't stick to the pot. The wontons are cooked after they have floated to the surface of the water and cooked for about 30 seconds. Remove the wontons and divide them between the bowls then finish with the spring onion.

There is nothing more comforting than a hot bowl of soup dumplings on a winter night. These dumplings, served in a soup made with chilli oil and dark vinegar, are a very popular street food from Shaanxi province, especially at the night markets there. This dish is very easy and quick to make.

酸湯水餃

SPICY SOUR SOUP DUMPLINGS

40 vegan dumplings (available from an Asian grocer)

2 garlic cloves, finely chopped

90 ml (3 fl oz) soy sauce

150 ml (5 fl oz) Chinese dark vinegar

90 ml (3 fl oz) Chilli oil (page 29)

1 teaspoon thirteen spice

2 teaspoons salt

2 nori sheets, broken into small pieces

2 spring onions (scallions), sliced

2 coriander (cilantro) stalks, cut into pieces

Bring 2 litres (68 fl oz/8 cups) water to the boil in a stockpot. Add the dumplings and stir so they don't stick to the pot. When the water comes back to the boil add 250 ml (8½ fl oz/1 cup) cold water. Stir carefully and, when the water boils again, the dumplings should be done. Remove the dumplings carefully with a sieve.

Divide the garlic, soy sauce, dark vinegar, chilli oil, thirteen spice, salt and nori between two bowls.

Divide the wontons equally between the bowls and add one soup ladle of the cooking water. Top with the spring onion and coriander.

This is another very delicious and simple dumpling dish.
The dumplings are covered in a sauce made with sesame paste,
chilli oil and other seasonings. It is very aromatic, intense and
satisfying.

廉墨水餃

SESAME PASTE DUMPLINGS

60 g (2 oz) Sesame paste/
sauce (page 49)

2 garlic cloves, finely chopped

3 tablespoons Chilli oil
(page 29)

½ teaspoon five spice
(see page 27)

2 tablespoons soy sauce

1 tablespoon Chinese dark
vinegar

1 spring onion (scallion), sliced

40 vegan dumplings

1 coriander (cilantro) stalk,
chopped

Divide the sesame paste, chopped garlic, chilli oil, five spice,
soy sauce, dark vinegar and spring onion between two bowls.

Bring 2 litres (68 fl oz/8 cups) water to the boil. Add the dumplings,
stirring regularly so they don't stick to the pot. When the water comes
back to the boil, add 250 ml (8½ fl oz/1 cup) cold water. Stir carefully,
and when the water boils again the dumplings should be done.
Remove the dumplings with a sieve and divide equally between the
two bowls. Mix everything together well and top with the coriander.

Baozi is a steamed bun with filling. You can basically fill the baozi with whatever you like, savoury or sweet. In this recipe I share how to make the buns from scratch as well as a delicious savoury filling. Once made, the baozi can be frozen and steamed again whenever you feel like it.

PREPARATION TIME
1 hour

COOKING TIME
30 minutes

SERVES
4

酸菜粉條灣

BAOZI FILLED WITH PICKLED CABBAGE AND SWEET POTATO NOODLES

In a large bowl, mix the yeast and flour with 240 ml (8 fl oz) water. Knead into a smooth dough. Cover the dough with a damp cloth and let it rest until it is one and a half times its original size. This might take 30 minutes or longer depending on the temperature.

Make the filling while the dough is resting. Heat a wok over a medium heat and, once hot, add the oil. Add the garlic and pickled chilli and stir for 30 seconds. Add the cabbage and sweet potato noodles, break them up with a spatula, then stir for 2–3 minutes. Add the soy sauce and vegan oyster sauce and stir for 1 minute. Add the sesame oil and turn off the heat.

Knead the dough quickly again and roll out with a rolling pin to get rid of the extra air. Cut the dough into sixteen portions and roll each portion into a round, thin wrap. The middle of the wrap should be slightly thicker than the edge so the baozi don't break easily.

Place a wrap in your palm. Place 1 tablespoon of the filling in the middle of the wrap and then use the thumb and index finger of your other hand to lift the edge of the wrap and carefully fold it, bit by bit, around the filling. You should be left with a bun shape that resembles a burger bun. Repeat with the remaining wraps and filling.

1 x 7 g (¼ oz) sachet instant dried yeast

500 g (1 lb 2 oz/3⅓ cups) plain (all-purpose) flour

3 tablespoons canola (rapeseed) oil

3 garlic cloves, chopped

6 pickled chillies (see page 31), chopped

250 g (9 oz) pickled cabbage, finely sliced

150 g (5½ oz) sweet potato noodles, soaked for 30 minutes then chopped

3 tablespoons soy sauce

1 tablespoon vegan oyster sauce

1 tablespoon sesame oil

Fill a saucepan with hot water and place a steam rack in the pot (the water level should not be higher than the steam rack). Place the buns on a plate on the steam rack, cover with a lid and steam over a high heat for 12 minutes. Turn off the heat but do not open the lid right away because the baozi will shrink if they come into sudden contact with cold air right after steaming. Let the baozi stay in the steaming pot for another 3–5 minutes before opening the lid. You may need to work in two batches.

Youtiao is the Chinese version of churros. Like Spanish churros, they are a very popular street food. The difference is that they are slightly salty and normally eaten at breakfast. Many people like to dip the fluffy, crunchy youtiao in congee or soy milk before eating them. They are sometimes used in cooking too, like in the famous Cantonese sampan congee, where small chunks of youtiao are cooked briefly with the congee.

油條

YOUTIAO

200 g (7 oz/1⅓ cups) plain (all-purpose) flour

½ teaspoon salt

480 ml (16 fl oz) canola (rapeseed) oil, plus 1 tablespoon extra and more for brushing

½ teaspoon bicarbonate of soda (baking soda)

1 teaspoon baking powder

145 ml (5 fl oz) plant-based milk

Mix the flour with the salt and 1 tablespoon of the oil in a bowl. Combine the bicarbonate of soda and baking powder in another bowl and add the milk. Mix well, then pour this mixture into the flour mixture and bring together into a dough. Remove from the bowl and knead until smooth, then return it to the bowl, cover with a damp tea towel (dish towel) and let it rest for 30 minutes.

Cut the dough in half and form each piece into a 20 cm (8 in) log. Brush a thin layer of oil over the logs, place in an airtight container and let them rest in the fridge overnight.

The next day, allow the dough to come to room temperature for 30 minutes. Then, with a rolling pin, gently roll the pieces into rectangles of 5 mm (¼ in) thickness.

Cut the flat dough into strips 3 cm (1¼ in) wide.

Add the oil to a frying pan and heat it over a high heat. Test the oil temperature with a wooden chopstick. When there are lots of little bubbles forming quickly around the chopstick that means the oil temperature is high enough. Reduce the heat to low.

Put one piece of dough on top of another. Press the dough lengthways with a chopstick, then remove the chopstick, take both ends of the youtiao with your hands and stretch it carefully to make it longer. Bring the ends of the dough together and press to join the ends, forming a loop. Repeat with the remaining strips of dough.

Carefully place the youtiao into the oil, working with one or two at a time. They will get bigger very quickly while frying, so use chopsticks to turn them carefully to fry the other side too. Take them out once golden. Normally it takes less than 30 seconds to fry each side.

DRINKS AND DESSERTS

There are so many good vegan Chinese drinks and desserts that I could write another book just about them. There are many great pastries made with wheat flour, rice flour, glutinous rice flour, wheat starch and so on that can be deep-fried, baked, steamed, made into different kinds of shapes and prepared in so many ways. But here I would like to focus mainly on the popular drinks and desserts that are typically served at a cha chaan teng (Hong Kong diner, 茶餐廳) or Cantonese dessert shop, which are mostly tea-based drinks with milk and some refreshing desserts based on mango and coconut cream. From Hong Kong milk tea to Mango pomelo sago, these are the things I grew up eating.

The bubble tea that has been booming in the last two decades is derived from the very long history of tea-drinking in China. Traditionally, tea has always been the most popular and common drink for most Chinese people. The quality and price can differ greatly between different teas, with the upper class able to afford the very refined tea made from a special harvest, and the lower class drinking the tea made from the coarse leaves of the tea plant.

In many southern regions where tea is produced, tea-drinking is an essential part of local life. In Cantonese, 'yum cha' literally means 'drinking tea'. It refers to going to a local restaurant (normally in the morning) to drink tea and eat dim sums. Many elderly Cantonese people do this as part of their morning routine. They just sit at the table and take their time to enjoy the tea and food while reading newspapers. At traditional restaurants in China, tea is always included by default. Customers pay a certain price per person and then have an endless supply of the tea of their choice during the meal.

In Fujian and the Chaoshan area of Guangdong province, the kung fu tea (工夫茶) ceremony is a daily routine of many people. The term means 'tea made with skills'. Ideally, spring water from the mountain is best for making kung fu tea. The ceremony is rather complicated and involves many tools. Essentially, the tea is brewed briefly in a very small purple clay teapot. Oolong tea is usually used and the leaf-to-water ratio is higher than in normal tea-making, so the tea is much stronger. The tea is then poured into small cups and has to be drunk quickly, otherwise it gets cold. After the tea is drunk, another round of tea-making and -drinking starts.

Talking and drinking tea together is what many friends and families do when they spend time with each other. The older generation usually prefers to drink pure tea, and the younger generation tends to choose bubble tea. Bubble tea is the drink I had most often in China, especially during school and university. We would always go out to get some bubble tea in our breaks.

Besides the common black tea, other kinds of tea can also be used in tea drinks, especially in fruit tea and bubble tea. If you are looking to make a refreshing fruit tea in summer, it is best to use a lighter tea, such as green tea or white tea. But if you are feeling like a warm tea drink with milk in winter, black tea would be the best option.

For Hong Kong–style tea drinks, Ceylon tea is normally used. In order to bring out the best aroma and taste in tea, many restaurants use a mixture of teas according to their fineness, based on a certain ratio. The whole tea leaves are used for their taste and aroma, the semi-fine tea is used to balance the taste, and the very fine tea is used to deepen the colour. To make the recipes here more accessible I have used only whole tea leaves and tea bags to make the tea.

Besides drinks, desserts should also not be missed while enjoying a great meal. Here, I am sharing some of the popular Hong Kong desserts made with mango, sago, coconut cream and milk, which are perfectly refreshing and light, to be served after a big meal. The mung bean cakes and fa gao can be kept longer and are ideal to gift and share with friends and family.

PREPARATION TIME
5 minutes

COOKING TIME
15 minutes

SERVES
2

If there is one drink that represents Hong Kong, it is Hong Kong–style milk tea. There is no sugar added to this fragrant milk tea, only evaporated milk. It is also called 'silk stocking milk tea' because the tea is filtered and pulled with a sackcloth bag that resembles a silk stocking. The tea is first cooked and pulled back and forth a few times, then cooked and pulled again. It is believed that the tea pulling helps to get rid of the bitter and grassy taste and to achieve a smoother texture.

Here, I use whole tea leaves and tea bags and a plant-based evaporated coconut milk. If you can't find any plant-based evaporated milk products, you can also cook your favourite plant-based milk over a low heat, and let it simmer for a few minutes until half of the milk has evaporated. The evaporation enhances the taste and smoothness of the milk.

港式奶茶

HONG KONG MILK TEA

10 g (¼ oz) Ceylon tea leaves

2 teabags Ceylon tea

180 ml (6 fl oz) plant-based evaporated milk

Boil 480 ml (16 fl oz) water in a saucepan and add the tea. When the water returns to the boil, reduce the heat to low and cook for 5 minutes then filter the tea leaves out using either a sackcloth bag (if you have one), a piece of muslin (cheesecloth) or a tea strainer.

Use a container to pull the tea, pouring it from a height first into the container then back into the pot four times.

Boil the tea again for 3 minutes, then pull it back and forth another four times.

If serving hot, fill two cups one-third of the way with the milk, then pour in the tea to fill the cups.

If served cold, first wait for the tea to cool down. Add ice cubes to a glass and enough plant-based evaporated milk to fill 30 per cent of the glass, then top up with the tea.

Iced lemon tea is one of the most popular and traditional drinks in Hong Kong. Like Hong Kong milk tea, it is served in every cha chaan teng, which you can find on basically every street in Hong Kong. Served with ice cubes, it is the perfect refreshing summer drink to share with friends.

凍檸茶

HONG KONG LEMON TEA

10 g (¼ oz) Ceylon tea leaves

2 teabags Ceylon tea

40 g (1½ oz) sugar

1 lemon

1 lime

12 ice cubes

Bring 480 ml (16 fl oz) water to the boil in a saucepan and add the tea. When the water returns to the boil, reduce the heat to low and cook the tea for 5 minutes, then filter the tea leaves out using either a sackcloth bag (if you have one), a piece of muslin (cheesecloth) or a tea strainer.

Use a container to pull the tea, pouring it from a height first into the container then back into the pot four times.

Add the sugar to the tea, mix it, then let it cool down. Meanwhile, cut the lemon and lime into 5 mm (¼ in) slices.

Add six slices of lemon and two slices of lime to a cocktail shaker, squeeze the juice out of one slice of lemon and use a muddler to smack the lemon and lime for 20 seconds, then add the tea, put on the lid and shake it hard for 30 seconds. If needed, you can divide the lemon, lime and tea in half and do this in two batches.

Add the ice cubes to two serving glasses and divide the tea and fruit between them.

PREPARATION TIME
5 minutes

COOKING TIME
15 minutes

SERVES
2

Yuenyeung is another traditional drink from Hong Kong. 'Yuenyeung' (鴛鴦) is the Cantonese name for 'mandarin duck', a kind of bird that almost always travels in pairs. Therefore, the bird's name is the same as 'lovebirds' in Chinese. When used in food, it refers to dishes that have two main ingredients or flavours, like this drink: a mixture of black tea and coffee. Another example is Yuanyang hot pot, which has two separate areas for spicy and non-spicy soup.

YUENYEUNG (COFFEE WITH TEA)

15 g (½ oz) Ceylon tea leaves

40 g (1½ oz) sugar

90 ml (3 fl oz) espresso

240 ml (8 fl oz) plant-based evaporated milk

Bring 480 ml (16 fl oz) water to the boil in a saucepan and add the tea. When the water returns to the boil, reduce the heat to low and cook the tea for 5 minutes, then filter the tea leaves out. Add the sugar and stir until it is dissolved.

Add the espresso and milk and mix well. This drink can be served warm or cold with ice cubes.

Bubble tea has definitely become the most popular drink in China for the last two decades, and tapioca pearls are an essential part of a good bubble tea. If you would like to make bubble tea at home, try making these tapioca pearls from scratch with only three ingredients.

PREPARATION TIME
20 minutes

COOKING TIME
10 minutes

SERVES
2

自製珍珠

TAPIOCA PEARLS

Dissolve 30 g (1 oz) of the sugar in the hot water, then add this mixture to a small saucepan. Heat it up over a low heat. Once the water boils, add 2 tablespoons of the tapioca starch and mix it together quickly with the water. Then add the rest of the tapioca starch, mixing continuously until all the liquid has been absorbed and you are left with a dough. Take the dough out and, wearing kitchen gloves, knead it immediately while it is still hot until it becomes smooth. If you don't have kitchen gloves, you can let it cool down for 1 or 2 minutes beforehand.

Cut the dough into three portions and roll each portion into a very long, thin rope. Cut each rope into small pieces, then roll each piece into a round to make pearls.

Bring 320 ml (11 fl oz) water to the boil with the remaining brown sugar in a saucepan over a medium–low heat. Once the water is boiling, add the tapioca pearls and cook for about 15 minutes, then turn off the heat, cover the pan with a lid and leave to sit for 15 minutes so the tapioca pearls can finish cooking in the residual heat.

You can store your tapioca pearls in their sugary liquid for up to 1 day, but after that they will get hard so it's best to eat them on the day they're made.

To store uncooked tapioca pearls, first roll them in tapioca starch so they don't stick together, then store in an airtight container in the fridge for up to 2 days before cooking them.

100 g (3½ oz) brown or black sugar

60 ml (2 fl oz/¼ cup) hot water

80 g (2¾ oz) tapioca starch

Iced adzuki beans (aka red bean ice) is a popular drink/dessert in Hong Kong. It's made with cooked and sweetened adzuki beans – which is also a dessert by itself – crushed ice and evaporated milk, and is sometimes also topped with ice cream.

紅豆冰

ICED ADZUKI BEANS

200 g (7 oz) dried adzuki beans

85 g (3 oz) crystal sugar

200 g (7 oz) ice cubes or crushed ice

480 ml (16 fl oz) plant-based evaporated milk

Soak the beans for 6 hours, then drain and store in an airtight container in the freezer overnight.

Bring 1 litre (34 fl oz/4 cups) water to the boil in a saucepan and add the frozen beans. When it comes back to the boil, add the sugar, cover with a lid and cook over a medium–low heat for about 1 hour, stirring occasionally and topping up with hot water if necessary.

When the beans are fully cooked but still more or less intact, turn off the heat and leave them to cool in the water. You can refrigerate the beans at this stage.

Drain the beans and divide them between four serving glasses to come about halfway up each glass. Top with the ice cubes until it fills about two-thirds of the glass, then top up with the milk.

PREPARATION TIME
20 minutes

COOKING TIME
10 minutes

SERVES
2

Mango sticky rice balls is a very popular dessert from Hong Kong. The fresh mango, the smooth coconut milk and the slightly chewy sticky rice balls make this a delicious and refreshing summer dessert. With only four ingredients and with no added sugar, it is easy to make and suits a variety of dietary preferences.

芒小丸子

MANGO STICKY RICE BALLS

120 g (4½ oz) glutinous rice flour

75 ml (2½ fl oz) hot water

3 ripe mangoes

180 ml (6 fl oz) plant-based milk

Mix the glutinous rice flour with the hot water, stirring everything together well with a spoon or chopsticks. After it has cooled down a little, knead it into a dough. Prepare a bowl of iced water.

Take a little of the dough at a time and roll it into a small ball. Or take a bigger piece of dough, roll it into a long rope and cut it into equal pieces then roll those pieces into balls. You can make them bigger or smaller depending on your preference.

Bring a saucepan of water to the boil and cook the rice balls, stirring regularly to prevent them sticking to the pan. They are cooked when they float to the surface. If the balls are about the size of tapioca pearls, they take about 3 minutes, but if they're larger they'll take a little longer. Remove with a sieve and immediately plunge into the iced water.

Peel the mangoes and cut the flesh into dice. Purée half of the dice with the plant-based milk in a blender. Divide the mango purée, rice balls and mango dice evenly between two serving bowls.

PREPARATION TIME
15 minutes

COOKING TIME
10 minutes

SERVES
2

Mango pomelo sago is the most classic mango dessert from Hong Kong. It is very fruity and refreshing, a perfect dessert for a summer night. It tastes better when it's served cold, and you can put all the ingredients (including the sago after it's cooked) in the fridge for an hour before mixing everything together.

楊枝甘露

MANGO POMELO SAGO

30 g (1 oz) sago

600 g (1 lb 5 oz) mango, peeled

240 ml (8 fl oz) coconut cream

90 ml (3 fl oz) plant-based milk

50 g (1¼ oz) pomelo flesh

Bring 480 ml (16 fl oz) water to the boil in a saucepan and cook the sago for 10 minutes over a medium–low heat, stirring regularly to prevent it sticking to the pan. Turn off the heat and cover with the lid. Leave the sago to finish cooking in the residual heat. It is properly cooked when it turns completely translucent. Drain.

Cut the mango into small dice and purée two-thirds of the dice.

Mix the coconut cream with the milk.

Divide the mixed milk, sago, mango purée, mango dice and pomelo between two serving bowls.

Lo mai chi is the Cantonese name for 'sticky rice balls', which are quite similar to mochi. A batter is first made with glutinous rice flour, cornflour (cornstarch) and milk, then it is steamed and becomes a dough. This dough is used to wrap fresh mango and then coated with coconut flakes. This is a great dessert to share with friends and family. It is best eaten on the day it is made, as it will become hard if stored in the fridge.

PREPARATION TIME
30 minutes

COOKING TIME
45 minutes

SERVES
2

芒果糯米糍

LO MAI CHI (STICKY RICE BALLS) FILLED WITH MANGO

Combine all the ingredients, except the coconut and mango, in a big shallow bowl. Mix until the batter is completely smooth.

Fill a saucepan with hot water and place a steam rack in the pot (the water level should not be higher than the steam rack). Place the batter on a plate on the steam rack, cover with a lid and let it steam over a high heat for 45 minutes. To check if the dough is cooked, insert a fork into the dough. If there is no liquid sticking to the fork, then the dough is cooked.

Remove the dough from the steamer and allow to cool down for a few minutes while you peel the mango. Cut the mango into 2 cm (¾ in) dice.

When the dough has cooled but is still quite warm, take a small portion (about 30 g/1 oz) at a time and, using gloves or brushing oil on your hands to prevent sticking, press the dough into a flat, round wrap that is thicker in the middle and thinner at the edges. Wrap the mango carefully, shaping the dough into a ball to enclose it, then coat the rice ball with dessicated coconut. Continue until all the dough is used up.

170 g (6 oz) glutinous rice flour
50 g (1¾ oz) cornflour (cornstarch)
70 g (2½ oz) sugar
180 ml (6 fl oz) coconut cream or milk
180 ml (6 fl oz) soy milk
30 g (1 oz) vegan butter or margarine
60 g (2 oz) dessicated coconut
600 g (1 lb 5 oz) mango

VEGAN CHINESE FOOD

Mung bean cake is a traditional Chinese pastry made with peeled mung beans. It is a good recipe if you want to make some small pastries for family and friends. It has a smooth and delicate taste, and it only requires four ingredients.

绿豆糕

MUNG BEAN CAKE

400 g (14 oz) peeled dried mung beans, soaked for 5 hours

60 ml (2 fl oz/¼ cup) canola (rapeseed) oil

100 g (3½ oz) sugar

50 g (1¾ oz) maltose or maple syrup

Bring a saucepan of water to the boil and cook the mung beans for 3 minutes, then drain.

Fill a saucepan with hot water and place a steam rack in the pot (the water level should not be higher than the steam rack). Place the mung beans on a plate on the steam rack, cover with a lid and let it steam over a high heat for 45 minutes. Once cooked, drain the beans then mash them with a spoon or a potato masher.

Add the oil to a non-stick frying pan set over the lowest possible heat. Add the mashed beans, sugar and maltose and stir until everything is combined together and the mixture has a smooth consistency.

Take about 50 g (1¾ oz) of the mung bean mixture and form it into the shape of a mooncake – about 4 cm (1½ in) wide and about 2–3 cm (¾–1¼ in) thick, like a very thick cookie. You can also use a mooncake mould to shape it. Continue until all the mixture has been used. The mung bean cakes can be stored in an airtight container in the fridge for up to 3 days.

PREPARATION TIME
45 minutes

COOKING TIME
30 minutes

MAKES
6

Fa gao is a steamed pastry from southern China. In many regions it is a festive food that is eaten during Chinese New Year. It is made with rice and sugar-tolerant yeast and has a similar consistency to cupcakes. Sugar-tolerant yeast is also called high-sugar yeast, and it depends on sugar to produce gas during the fermentation process. It is used when the sugar accounts for 8 to 30 per cent of the flour weight. Low-sugar yeast might become inactive in foods that contain a high amount of sugar.

发糕

FA GAO (SPONGE RICE CAKE)

| 300 g (10½ oz) rice flour |
| 60 g (2 oz) plain (all-purpose) flour |
| 60 g (2 oz) sugar |
| 5 g (⅛ oz) sugar-tolerant yeast |
| 320 ml (11 fl oz) plant-based milk |

Add all of the ingredients to a bowl and mix well until a smooth batter forms. Cover the bowl and let the batter rest until it doubles in size. This step might take 30 minutes to 1 hour, depending on the temperature.

Stir the batter again for 1–2 minutes to get rid of any big bubbles inside. Pour the batter into six cupcake moulds until each is about 80 per cent full. Do not fill the moulds completely as the cake will expand during steaming.

Fill a saucepan with hot water and place a steam rack in the pot (the water level should not be higher than the steam rack). Place the cupcake moulds on a plate on the steam rack, cover with a lid and let it steam over a high heat for 30 minutes. Turn off the heat. Leave the fa gao in the steaming pot for another 5 minutes before opening the lid. Best enjoyed when eaten warm.

INDEX

S

T

ABOUT THE AUTHOR

Yang Liu was born in Hunan province in China and spent her early years moving around China, sampling all the different cuisines in each region. Eight years ago, she moved to Spain, where she met her partner, Katharina Pinczolits, and the two now live in Austria. Together, they became vegan and started exploring and experimenting with vegan Chinese cuisine. They started their Instagram account, littlericenoodle, in late 2019 and have since accumulated over 165,000 followers, who love watching their videos of how to make vegan Chinese food.

Published in 2024 by Hardie Grant Books, an imprint of Hardie Grant Publishing

Hardie Grant Books (Melbourne)
Wurundjeri Country
Building 1, 658 Church Street
Richmond, Victoria 3121

Hardie Grant Books (London)
5th & 6th Floors
52–54 Southwark Street
London SE1 1UN

hardiegrant.com/books

Hardie Grant acknowledges the Traditional Owners of the Country on which we work,
the Wurundjeri People of the Kulin Nation and the Gadigal People of the Eora Nation,
and recognises their continuing connection to the land, waters and culture. We pay our
respects to their Elders past and present.

 A catalogue record for this
book is available from the
National Library of Australia

Vegan Chinese Food
ISBN 978 1 74379 936 9

10 9 8 7 6 5 4 3 2 1

Commissioning Editor: Rushani Epa
Managing Editor: Loran McDougall
Project Editors: Emily Hart and Antonietta Melideo
Editor: Andrea O'Connor
Design Manager: Kristin Thomas
Designer: George Saad
Production Manager: Todd Rechner

Colour reproduction by Splitting Image Colour Studio
Printed in China by Leo Paper Products LTD.

 The paper this book is printed on is from FSC®-certified forests
and other sources. FSC® promotes environmentally responsible,
socially beneficial and economically viable management of the
world's forests.